Reading After Theory

Blackwell Manifestos

In this new series major critics make timely interventions to address important concepts and subjects, including topics as diverse as, for example: Culture, Race, Religion, History, Society, Geography, Literature, Literary Theory, Shakespeare, Cinema, and Modernism. Written accessibly and with verve and spirit, these books follow no uniform prescription but set out to engage and challenge the broadest range of readers, from undergraduates to postgraduates, university teachers and general readers – all those, in short, interested in ongoing debates and controversies in the humanities and social sciences.

Published

The Idea of Culture
Terry Eagleton

The Future of Christianity
Alister E. McGrath

Reading After Theory
Valentine Cunningham

21st-Century Modernism: The "New" Poetics
Marjorie Perloff

Forthcoming

The Death of Race
David Goldberg

The Future of Society
William Outhwaite

The Future of Theory
Jean-Michelle Rabate

The Idea of Black Culture
Hortense Spillars

Post/Modern Religion
Graham Ward

Reading After Theory

Valentine Cunningham

First published 2002

2 4 6 8 10 9 7 5 3 1

Blackwell Publishers Ltd
108 Cowley Road
Oxford OX4 1 JF
UK

Blackwell Publishers Inc
350 Main Street
Malden, Massachusetts 02148
USA

British Library Cataloguing in Publication Data

A CIP catalogue record for this book is available from the British Library.

Library of Congress Cataloging-in-Publication Data

Cunningham, Valentine.
    Reading after theory / Valentine Cunningham.
        p.   cm. — (Blackwell manifestos)
    Includes index.
    ISBN 0-631-22167-0 (alk. paper) — ISBN 0-631-22168-9 (pbk. : alk. paper)
    1. Criticism—20th century.   2. Literature, Modern—History and criticism.
I. Title.   II. Series.

PN94 .C86 2002
801'.95'0904—dc21
                                                                    2001004521

Typeset in 11½ on 13½ pt Bembo
by Ace Filmsetting Ltd, Frome, Somerset
Printed in Great Britain by MPG Books, Bodmin, Cornwall

This book is printed on acid-free paper.

Metaphisics is a word, that you, dear Sir! are no great
Friend to / but yet you will agree, that a great Poet must
be, implicitè if not explicitè, a profound Metaphysician.
He may not have it in logical coherence, in his Brain &
Tongue; but he must have it by *Tact* / for all sounds, &
forms of human nature he must have the *ear* of a wild
Arab listening in the silent Desart, the eye of a North
American Indian tracing the footsteps of an Enemy
upon the Leaves that strew the Forest – the *Touch* of a
Blind Man feeling the face of a darling Child –

(Samuel Taylor Coleridge,
writing to William Sotheby, 15 July 1802)

Contents

1

What Then? What Now?

But louder sang that ghost, 'What then?'

W. B. Yeats, 'What Then?'

It's the voice of Plato's ghost in the Yeats poem 'What Then?' ' "What then?" sang Plato's ghost. "What then?" ' The poet climbs higher and higher, his career and fame more and more magnificent, but still the nagging question comes, 'What then?'

> 'The work is done,' grown old he thought,
> 'According to my boyish plan;
> Let the fools rage, I swerved in naught,
> Something to perfection brought';
> *But louder sang that ghost, 'What then?'*

And so it is with literary theory. After so much theorizing the question still remains: What then? What now? What do we readers do, what should we do, what might we do, in the wake – the huge wake – of theory? Or Theory, as I shall call it, with a capital letter, to signify the modern kind which took over from the 1960s on. The late Paul de Man, the extremely influential Yale Deconstructionist, used to suggest that the only critical task left to us after Theory – after his kind of Theory – would be the steady rereading of all the literary canon, all the texts which had been read earlier and otherwise, but deconstructively. Deconstruction was to be criticism's final word, its Final Solution. De Man was by no means the first to believe that criticism's

1

endgame had arrived. Earlier in the twentieth century the New Critics and their disciples acted as if the only way forward then for criticism was turning every poem into a well-wrought urn or verbal icon according to these critics' special dicta. That did not last; and neither did Paul de Man's wish for the future of criticism. Mr de Man, he dead; to coin a phrase. He died in political ignominy and intellectual disgrace, bringing to an abrupt end the short story, or reading bandwagon, of Yale Deconstruction – or at least Paul de Man's version of it. What then? What now? cried the ghost of all those writers and writings de Man had crammed with fearsome asperity into the theorized maw of his analyses. And the ghosts of all those texts de Man's allies and pupils had busily deconstructed, and the ghosts of all the ones waiting in the wings to be de-Manned by the man himself, joined in.

Reading would go on; it must go on (hear the ghost of Beckett's Unnameable saying so); it goes on. For better or worse, though, reading cannot ignore Theory, because reading can never ignore its pre-history; and it certainly can't ignore the kind of Theory which Paul de Man represented, and all the other close relations of it, all the critical twists and turns coming from and through the so-called 'linguistic turn'. I'm very sure that Theory, not all of it, perhaps, but great parts of it, Theory in the main, certainly the impact of Theory, is, like 'our love' in the song, 'here to stay'. But the question is: So what? What to do with it, and in the tumultuous aftermath of it? What Then? What Now?

2

Reading Always Comes After

Samuel Sharp said, 'I never did understand that word'. I said it meant that I'd assimilated feminism without being obsessed by it. He said, with a roguish smile, 'Oh, then, I'm a post-feminist too'. I said that the treatment of women in his screenplays made that hard to believe.

David Lodge, *Home Truths: A Novella*

Reading always comes after theory. We all, as readers, trail behind theory, theory of some kind or another. We are all, always, post-theory, post-theorists. The question for us always is: What then? What follows? What do we do as readers in consequence of this persistent and normal belatedness? This has always been the question since theorizing about literature began two-and-a-half millennia or so ago, with Plato and Aristotle. It's even more urgently the question now, with the great contemporary avalanche, the Niagara torrent, of literary theorizing. It's the question of this book – which is by no means a mere paean of praise to theory, especially not to Theory, but is not a mere jeremiad either. It's certainly not wanting to join the chorus of mere whingers against Theory, all those mouthy conservatives from (say) Helen Gardner, *In Defence of the Imagination* (1982) to Roger Shattuck, *Candor and Perversion* (1999), with their romps up and down the glooming critical slopes of the Blooms, Alan and Harold.

The poet Philip Larkin, wearing his other hat as jazz critic, once began a review by invoking his favourite opposition between the progressive optimist H. G. Wells and the gloomier Edward (*Decline and*

3

Fall) Gibbon, and saying that 'the jazz historian is usually either a Wells or a Gibbon: either things are growing better and better, or they are getting progressively worse'. Which nicely describes discussion about literary theory, and about Theory especially. Larkin went on: 'Since the music seems to be suffering a radical upheaval every twenty years or so, there is plenty of evidence for either side'.[1] Which has force for the state of literary theory, particularly in the recent Theory years. This book likes to think it is on the side of both Wells and of Gibbon.

Reading is inevitably belated. It's always posterior work. It obviously comes after writing. It needs the already written, some given textual material, to precede it. In that clear sense reading is supplementary. But it's also, if slightly less obviously, a supplement to theory and theories. The reader, and so also the reading, always arrive in some sense preformed, prejudging, prejudiced, predisposed, by ideas about how reading is done, and what to expect from the kind of text which is presented, what to expect from any text. It would in any case be odd if readers would even want to shed their prejudices, their beliefs, the attitudes that form them and their reading opinions, all the mishmash of notions and assumptions garnered in from their upbringing and education and just being-in-the-world, the key components of their selfhood, in other words, the things that make up their uniqueness as persons, just because they are sitting down with a book. It's difficult to imagine readers being able to wipe their intellectual and emotional and imaginative and ethical and spiritual slate clean even if they wished to do so. All readers arrive at the book, the page, simply laden with presuppositional baggage, much of which is, inevitably, of a literary-theoretical kind.

In fact, it's hard to see how reading could proceed without this luggage. Jonathan Culler has talked very aptly in his book *Structuralist Poetics* (1974), borrowing a notion from Noam Chomsky's linguistics, of the readerly *competences* we all must bring to bear when we start to read a new text. To get on with reading a work we have to know how to proceed with it. Different sorts of book, text, novel, poem, and so forth, require different reading strategies, practices, competences.

Readers get used to looking out, as they enter a text, for signs to indicate which particular competences to bring into play. We do it, often, without thinking. It can be catastrophic, as well as tragicomic, or comical, or simply wrong, if you try to read your travel book as if it were a novel, an epic as if it were an elegy, a cookbook as if it were a volume of poems. Some texts, of course, don't let you come to easy decisions, they keep you guessing a lot. How, say, do you read the Bible? And writers and texts like playing games with their readers. That cookbook really is a volume of poems; that autobiography is posing as a novel; this novel is pretending to be a travel book. And so on. Many texts happily switch genres, and make you draw on a whole bank of competences. But the point for now is that any reading depends on your knowing something of how to proceed in doing it. The unprepared reader gets nowhere, or not very far.

A reader has to be, by definition, forewarned and forearmed; is always a bearer of earlier knowledge and knowledges; is always in some sense already fallen into knowledge. Reading is always a postlapsarian business. It has always eaten of the tree of theoretical knowledge. So it is never innocent. It simply cannot exist unschooled. We are all taught to read, in the sense of grasping the mere mechanics of this doing; and then we're taught to read, to make sense of what we're 'reading', taught how to make meaning, to make sense of it. This latter happens so early for some of us, and so discreetly for lots of us, that we didn't notice at the time that we were being so instructed. Which is ideology and belief for you: they creep up on you, they have crept up on you, usually, you scarcely knew, scarcely know, how.

There is, of course, a common fantasy of the independent, the natural reader, of men and women quite alone with the text, making sense of it by their own unaided efforts, uncontaminated by givens and pre-suppositions, by prejudices and doctrines, especially not anything that might be called theory, or (especially) Theory. This dream fires many a whinge against current literary education. But no one ever did read *de novo*, raw, naturally; understanding never came that easily. No reading-scene in history or fiction or any other art – and literature heavily bombards the reader with scenes of reading: the prevalence of such exempla, especially in novels and poems, is yet one more indication of the sheer inescapability of instructions to readers about how to pursue this activity – no reading-scene you can find anywhere in print or paint or any other medium in fact supports an absence of guidance or the need for guidance in the making sense of writing. And this is true even when it's being suggested that reading is an activity which is to be conducted simply as a transaction between an open book and a reader absolutely on his or her own, doing reading simply for himself or herself, in other words as a participant in the central Western myth of the free individual self and the Open Book.

The long Christian tradition of saving-encounters with the biblical text frequently implies that meaningful revelation will come from a quite individual encounter with the greatest case of the Open Book, the Judaeo-Christian sacred text, the Big Book of God, the Bible. The famous story of St Augustine's conversion, for instance, became a *locus classicus* among highly individualistic Protestants as a model of how all you needed was to come simply and openly to the Bible, and enlightenment and understanding would inevitably follow. In his garden in Milan in the summer of 386, this unhappy Professor of Rhetoric had his whole life changed when he overheard a child's voice singing a song whose refrain was *tolle, lege* – 'take (it) up and read' – and he duly picked up St Paul's Epistle to the Romans, opened the book at random at chapter 13, and read verses 13 and 14: 'Let us walk honestly, as in the day; not in rioting and drunkenness, not in chambering and wantonness, not in strife and envying. But put ye on the Lord Jesus Christ, and make no provision for the flesh, to fulfil the lusts thereof.' 'I had no wish to read any more and no need to do so', Augustine tells us in his *Confessions*. 'For in an instant, as I came to the end of the sentence, it was as though the light of confidence flooded into my heart and all the darkness of doubt was dispelled.'[2] It's one of the great reading encounters: an example to the whole Christian era; its exemplary force truly mythic for Western consciousness and assumptions about readers and reading. The Word speaks, and clearly, to its unaided reader; mere receptivity is all that's called for; take up the book without prejudice, read it without prejudice, and you will

6

get its message. And these are the classic Christian and Western assumptions taken from such exemplary encounters – ones deemed foundational to the whole era of what Derrideans rightly dub logocentrism.

John Milton's approach to the Bible in his *De Doctrina Christiana*, the *Christian Doctrine* (named after Augustine's work of the same title), endorses this vision in what is one of the great uncompromising statements of the responsibilities and privileges of the unindoctrinated reading individual. Christian believer-readers are to read the bare Word (*sola scriptura*, the scripture alone) and all on their own; that's all that is needed to find out the rules and the canons of the faith. 'Every believer is entitled to interpret the scriptures; and by that I mean interpret them for himself'; 'no one else can usefully interpret them for him'. The Christian reader is envisioned as always on his own, following his own conscience, utterly unaided by the 'visible church', its doctors, priests, canonical authorities, or by the magistrate, the agent of the state.[3]

This is the view of the reading process which animates the very Protestant story of Robinson Crusoe – the isolated reader all alone on his uninhabited island with only the plain, unannotated pages of the Bible before him (he has, in fact, threes copies of the book to choose from), and reading his way into salvation, the solo seeker for meaning in an encounter with the mere book, unassisted by priest or church or commentator, and finding truth, *sola scriptura*, by the reading of scripture, the writing, alone.

> How infinite and inexpressible a Blessing it is, that the Knowledge of God and of the Doctrine of Salvation by *Christ Jesus*, is so plainly laid down in the Word of God; so easy to be receiv'd and understood: That as the bare reading of the Scripture made me capable of understanding enough of my Duty to carry me directly on to the great Work of sincere Repentance for my Sins, and laying hold of a Saviour for Life and Salvation, to a stated Reformation in Practice, and Obedience to all God's Commands, and this without any Teacher or Instructor, I mean, humane . . . so the plain Instruction. . . .[4]

7

Plainly laid down in the Word of God; bare reading; without any teacher or instructor; plain instruction: the Protestant claim is clear. But, of course, there are pre-instructions, plenty of them. At the level of metaphysical resource, of course, in the Christian believer's invocation of God's help towards understanding – in St Augustine's repeated stress on divine mercy, or grace, or the coaching from God; in Milton's declared reliance on the Holy Spirit, 'who guides truth', and on the mind of Christ to steer the otherwise solo reader; in Defoe's parenthetical recall that, after all, he had a non-human teacher or instructor. And obviously these triumphant readers had much more by way of backing than even their pious claims on Holy Spirit guidance are allowing. Augustine was by no means a naive reader when he picked up the Epistle to the Romans. The Professor of Rhetoric was a deep reader of the classics. Chapter 8 of the *Confessions*, 'The Birthpangs of Conversion', is a story of much doctrinal alerting and preparatory working toward that crucial moment of understanding. From the learned Simplicianus he'd heard all about the Christian readings of the Platonic writings he knew, and how the African rhetor Marius Victorinus had learned to read the Bible savingly. Inspired by this, Augustine had taken to reading St Paul for himself, to the surprise of a Christian visitor, Ponticianus, when he found St Paul's writings open 'on top a gaming table'; and Ponticianus told him a friend had been inspired to a change of life by reading a Life of St Antony; and Augustine recalls how aged eighteen he'd read Cicero's *Hortensius* and 'been stirred to a zeal for wisdom'. Mightily guilty, too, about his worldliness, his desires, his sex life, Augustine was primed for a result from reading Romans 13. He knew full well what to expect from the reading of good books – especially Christian ones, especially St Paul – by way of personal moral reformative effect. And lo and behold, that effect occurred. The Holy Spirit had, so to say, an already instructed reader to instruct. And so too with Milton, the most widely and deeply instructed reader of the Bible there has, perhaps, ever been. Milton, who, even in the *De Doctrina*, invokes traditional Christian hermeneutic assumptions and practices:

The right method of interpreting the scriptures has been laid down by theologians. This is certainly useful. . . . The requisites are linguistic ability, knowledge of the original sources, consideration of the overall intent, distinction between literal and figurative language, examination of the causes and circumstances, and of what comes before and after the passage in question, and comparisons of one text with another.

The solo reader is, in practice, to be armed, then, with a panoply of established interpretative rules – the distinction between literal and figurative meaning, for example – as well as extra-textual knowledge, about original manuscripts of the text, its manuscript 'sources'. This reader is formidably predisposed as reader – in keeping with Milton's traditional invocation of 'the analogy of faith'. 'It must always be asked, too, how far the interpretation is in agreement with faith' ('*fideiquoque analogia ubique spectanda est*': 'too, the analogy of faith must be observed, or looked out for, even *inspected*, everywhere in the text'). The 'analogy of faith' was something like the common denominators of Christian belief, derived from and expressed in the whole body of ascertained scriptural meaning and the creeds, i.e. the givens of main Christian doctrine, what we would certainly ascribe to 'theory'. And this check on reading provided by the analogy of faith was, I'd say, undoubtedly part of what Milton meant by the believing reader having 'the mind of Christ'.[5]

As for Robinson Crusoe, his responses to the Bible text are all of them the given, classically Protestant and Puritan ones, based in the Nonconformist education in Bible reading his author Daniel Defoe was steeped in, and which, it would appear, after all, that Crusoe himself, for all his pose as the merely naive opener of the Bible's pages, knows a great deal about. From the beginning of Crusoe's narrative, as his disobedience to his father's 'serious and excellent Counsel' turns him into a modern Prodigal Son, he's actually caught up in reenactments of biblical narratives, an example of the Puritan reading expectation that the text of the Bible will come alive, will be reperformed in everyday living. Right from the start, Crusoe comes to us as a knowing Bible reader. The insistence on doing without human instructedness is itself a sign of how deeply instructed he is in current debates about the nature of the Bible text, its reading, and its role in Christian initiation and guidance. And what Crusoe goes on to say about himself and Man Friday – another plain reader of the Bible on the model of Crusoe himself – simply confirms his large access to current theological and biblical controversy:

> As to all the Disputes, Wranglings, Strife, and Contention which has happen'd in the World about Religion, whether Niceties in Doctrines, *or* Schemes of Church Government, they were all perfectly useless to us. . . . We had the *sure Guide* to Heaven, *viz.*, the Word of God; and we had, *blessed be God*, comfortable Views of the Spirit of God, teaching us and instructing us by His Word, *leading us into all Truth*, and making us both willing and obedient to the Instruction of his Word.

Crusoe the reader arrives at his reading, in other words, after threading his way through wrangling precisely about Bible meanings; he possesses comforting views about how biblical meaning is arrived at. He's a guided man. And – to repeat – how could he otherwise manage to make sense of his opened Book, his chosen text?

The Bible story of St Philip's encounter with a Jewish Ethiopian eunuch is most explicit about this prior requirement. Leaving Samaria (Acts 8), Philip catches up with this Treasurer of Ethiopian Queen Candace who is on his way home from Jerusalem by chariot. The official is having read to him aloud a scroll of Isaiah. He's at Isaiah chapter 53, verses 7 and 8, when Philip overhears the reading – verses about the death of the Suffering Servant. 'Understandest thou what thou readest?' Philip asks. 'And he said, "How can I, except some man should guide me?"' There will be no solitary understanding. Philip gets up into the chariot – the ready respondent to the textual enigmatic. 'Of whom speaketh the prophet thus? Of himself or of some other man?' asks the eunuch. A Christological reading is promptly offered. 'Then Philip opened his mouth, and began at the same scripture, and preached unto him Jesus.' The eunuch accepts this interpretation, believes with all his heart on the Christ of the reading, and is baptized at the very next watering-hole. The lesson is clear: effective comprehension, properly performed, indeed performative reading, only comes from somebody on hand to guide as reading's First Aider. Every Theseus needs an Ariadne and her ball, her *clew* no less, of handy thread, her well-spun theoretical yarn, so to say, interpretative clues in fact (*clew/clue*: they're the same word) to help him into and out of the labyrinths, the mazes, of meaning. An Ariadne's guidance is the only way to clued-up reading, the only way of preventing the eunuch's continuing amazement over the text – amazement being the discomfiting state of being stuck in the interpretative maze, mazed, confused, amazed.

It's the realization embedded in one of fiction's most touching scenes of reading – the story of how poverty-stricken Maggie Tulliver in George Eliot's *The Mill on the Floss* (1860) learns a necessary lesson of personal renunciation by reading St Thomas à Kempis's *The Imitation of Christ* in an old copy given her by her good friend the unbookish Bob Jakin. From this chance encounter with a written voice from the past Maggie finds deep ethical consolation and guidance (the chapter in which it occurs, book 4, chapter 3, is entitled 'A Voice from the Past'). But when she takes up the book she doesn't find its most helpful places all by herself – they're pointed out by somebody else's having turned down certain page-corners and made marks on the page. Maggie's reading has been preceded by another's; it is, as ever, posterior to someone else's; to be an effective reader she stands, and, I repeat, instructively so, in need of help.

> She took up the little, old, clumsy book with some curiosity: it had the corners turned down in many places, and some hand, now forever quiet, had made at certain passages strong pen-and-ink marks, long since browned by time. Maggie turned from leaf to leaf, and read where the quiet hand pointed. . . .
> 'Know that the love of thyself doth hurt thee more than anything in the world . . .'

A strange thrill of awe passed through Maggie while she read, as if she had been wakened in the night by a strain of solemn music, telling of beings whose souls had been astir while hers was in stupor. She went on from one brown mark to another, where the quiet hand seemed to point. . . .[6]

The 'common reader now requires mediation to read *Paradise Lost* with full appreciation', Harold Bloom has recently told us, with evident nostalgia for a time when, he's suggesting, little or no such mediation was needed.[7] I doubt whether such a time ever existed. Certainly we're all Ethiopian eunuchs and Maggie Tullivers nowadays – we all need somebody to guide us, an explicatory Philip, some pointing hand. The Law, declares the biblical writer to the Galatians (3: 24), 'was our schoolmaster to bring us unto Christ, that we might be justified by faith'. No knowledge without a 'schoolmaster', then. Schoolmaster, pedagogue, *paidagogos*: he was the slave in Greek households whose job was escorting boys to school. All readers, all readings, must – the whole tradition of reading shouts out – be taken to school. Literary theory is a main lesson being offered there.

3

Theory, What Theory?

To read on a system . . . is very apt to kill what it suits us to consider the more humane passion for pure and disinterested reading.

Virginia Woolf, 'Hours in a Library'

We all – all of us readers – come after theory. Certainly. But what theory? It's commonly said and assumed that we've lived through a theory revolution in the last few decades. And this is correct. We live within an abundance of apparently novel theories, approaches, terminology, rhetorics. Theory is everywhere. Certainly it's rare to find anywhere now a published discussion or reading of literature, or to hear a lecture on a literary topic, certainly by a professional critic from the academy, which doesn't deploy critical terms which were quite unknown before, say, 1965, and which is not paying homage to named theorists of literature who might well have been writing before then but were known only to a few close-up chums and colleagues. A critical Rip Van Winkle waking up now after fifty years of slumber wouldn't recognize the critical tower of Babel he'd returned to. Cynics think that literary studies have always been too much in love with neologisms, because we're all a bunch of pseudo-scientists desperate for a rationale for our work and so always on the *qui vive* for highfalutin important-sounding terminologies to dazzle and confute our critics and opponents with. If that is even nearly so, then the last few decades will have been peculiarly satisfying for insiders, for the literary-critical business simply bristles now with critical neologisms,

13

our readerly sky quite brilliantly alight with rhetorical bravado. Our Theory lexicon certainly puts on a good show. Or a bad one, if you're one of Theory's many enemies. (The terminological sword swings both ways.)

You can easily spot 'postmodernist' departments of literature, says the conservative US National Association of Scholars, if their Course Catalogues use any items from a list of 115 deplorable Theory items the Association (www.nas.org) has helpfully drawn up. This long, shiny hit-list includes: agency, AIDS, Baudrillard, bodies, canonicity, Chomsky, cinematic, classism, codes, color, contextualism, decentered, Deleuze, de Man, Derrida, discourse, dominant, erotic, eurocentric, feminism, feminisms, feminist, Foucault, Freud, Freudian, gay, gayness, gaze, gender, gendered, Guattari, gynocentric, hegemon, hegemonic, heteronormative, heterosexism, historicist, homoeroticism, identity, ideology, imperialism, incest, Lacan, lesbian, lesbianism, logocentric, Lyotard, maleness, marginalized, Marxism, modernism, oppression, otherness, patriarchal, patrimony, phallocentric, postcolonialism, postmodernism, poststructuralism, power, praxis, psychosexual, queer, queered, queering, race, sex, sexism, sexualities, slavery, structuralism, subaltern, subjectivism, theory, transgendered, transsexual, voice, whiteness, womanism, womyn.[1]

Merrily listing sixty of the NAS's terms, the London *Times Literary Supplement* (6 October 2000) chortled that you should apply to the colleges which evinced 'the highest percentage' of such 'postmodern' terminology 'if this makes your brain cells shine with delight'. But both the NAS and the *TLS* are missing the point; the historical point. For these terms and approaches to literature, the reading interests they suggest and promote, are simply everywhere in university departments of English and of other literatures, and in faculties and sub-faculties devoted to studies, such as Cultural Studies, which also use literature as evidence and certainly encourage the 'reading' of social 'texts' as an investigative method. They're normal and normative. Contemporary reading, certainly as that is attempted in universities, cannot, apparently, do without them – and many more of their ilk.

Theory of the kinds indicated by the NAS list – what I'm calling

14

Theory with a capital T – is simply ubiquitous. Much of what comes under this title is not, of course, strictly speaking, theoretical – at least not in a scientific sense of a proposition, a model, a theorem, a description telling you in a testable, provable–disprovable fashion what literature and the literary are and how they or one or other of their branches function. But then poems, novels, genres of literature, are not like an enzyme, say, or an atomic sub-particle, or a chemical element, nor even like moons or that large rambling entity the human body (even though 'body' is, of course, a favourite metaphor for literary things: 'body of writings', we say; 'body of work'; 'in the body of the text'; and so on), so perhaps we would be simply wrong to expect theories of the literary to function as do scientific cognitive instruments, models, theorems, mathematical symbols and equations. Which doesn't stop many Theorists wanting this scientificism. Some achieve something like it. The closer to linguistics the Theorist operates the more possible and convincing this is. The linguistic parts and structures and functions of writing – a dental fricative, it might be, or a phoneme, a dative, a signifier, a sentence – are not dissimilar in their knowability and boundedness to particles or moons, objects whose nature and behaviour can be identified and predicted and truly theorized. It's quite a bit otherwise with Satire, or the Novel, or the Sixteenth Century.

   Much of what is offered as literary theory, and Theory especially, poses as a set of genetic codes for literature, as what Gerard Genette has called a 'constitutive' or 'essentialist' poetics, as what E. D. Hirsch means by a 'general hermeneutics'. But in practice most 'theory', and Theory not least, comes down to what Stanley Fish has called mere rules of thumb, or Genette's 'conditionalist poetics', i.e. temporarily useful lines and avenues of reading approach, utilities of interpretation, simple practices of criticism (as Fish has suggested), principles of reading, mere matters of belief, of hunch even – the mess of useful assumptions I happen to have in my critical kitbag, postures and practices driven by contingency and pragmatism as much as by necessity, sometimes even downright blagues and try-ons, things the 'theorist' has just thought of.[2]

15

Theorists don't like the charge of untheoretical messiness, and work hard to disprove it. Some have tried to lean on etymology for the strict meaning of their work, and invoke the originating Greek word *theoros*, spectator. So theory becomes spectator work, what onlookers and audiences do. And of course much Theory has invoked the defining authority and presence of 'the interpretive community' and 'reader responses' and invoked various sorts of readerly 'gaze' as fixable markers of the pursuit. But such invocations remain as slippery and elusive as so much else that interests Theorists, and they keep failing to harden up into the tough objects of the would-be scientific gaze their deployers crave. Indeed thinking of theory/Theory as a kind of spectator sport does rather give the game away. What precisely is an interpretive community? It's just one very loose cannon of a notion knocking about the Theoretical field. And loose cannons generate loose canons of Theory – more conditionalist than constitutive, to use Genette's distinction. Literary theorizing is generally at some remove from what the German vocabulary claims is *Literaturwissenschaft*, literary science. And this is so even when so-called scientists are attempting the theorizing. The psychiatrist Jacques Lacan, one of the modern masters of Theory, presented his literary theorizings as part and parcel of his scientific work, and his pages come littered with algebra, algorithms, seeking to express functions of language, and cognition, and so of reading. But that doesn't grant his speculations and his concepts theoretical status in a way an astrophysicist or a biochemist would recognize (which is, of course, as much a problem for psychiatry as for literary criticism).

But still we talk of theory, and I will talk of Theory. Notwithstanding the looseness of the term, vague, ultra-compendious, a huge flag of convenience, it has stuck, and in practice we know more or less what it covers. It does indeed comprise the loose assemblage of concerns and positions evinced by the NAS list, and the allied assumptions the list implies. We all know what it means. It has indeed come to mean what Jonathan Culler had more or less in mind when, back in 1983 in his book *On Deconstruction*, he suggested that 'theory' *tout court* would be an apter label for contemporary literary business than 'literary theory', and that 'theory' was now a recognizable genre, and that 'reading as a woman', say, would be a main way of 'doing' theory, of entering into the essence of this 'genre'.

What's embraced by the label theory, what I mean by Theory, is what you expect to find and indeed do find in those proliferating university courses called 'Theory' or 'Introductions to Theory'; what you find in the exploding field of handy student handbooks and text-books with titles like Raman Selden's *A Reader's Guide to Contemporary Literary Theory* (1985, 1989), or his *Practising Theory and Reading Literature* (1989), or Andrew Bennett and Nicholas Royle's *An Introduction to Literature, Criticism and Theory: Key Critical Concepts* (1995), or Julian Wolfreys's *Literary Theories: A Reader and Guide* (1999). It's what concerns the burgeoning number of encyclopedias such as Irena Makaryk's lovely, fat *Encyclopedia of Contemporary Literary Theory: Approaches, Scholars, Terms* (1993), or Jeremy Hawthorn's *A Glossary of Contemporary Literary Theory* (1992). The scope is, of course, Structuralism and Feminism and Marxism and Reader-Response and Psychoanalysis and Deconstruction and Poststructuralism and Post-modernism and New Historicism and Postcolonialism – the concerns of the various sections of the Wolfreys volume, in the order in which they appear. The modern gurus of Theory on these lines are, of course, the likes of Mikhail Mikhailovich Bakhtin, Walter Benjamin, Roland Barthes, Louis Althusser, Jacques Derrida, Paul de Man, Jacques Lacan, Julia Kristeva, Luce Irigaray, Michel Foucault, non-anglophone thinkers all, but most notably French-speakers, the French men and women who poured the Word from Paris (as John Sturrock has aptly put it)[3] into eager anglophone ears from the 1960s onwards. (A key historical moment of delighted encounter and cultural insertion can even be dated exactly to the conference in 1966 at Johns Hopkins University intended to introduce French structuralism into the North American academy, when what turned up in practice was poststructuralism, in-cluding the momentously influential Jacques Derrida with his deconstructive vision of reading as a game forever poised between 'two interpretations of interpretation' – on the one hand the weary old logocentric quest for meaning as truth, and on the other the zippier new expectation of meaning as imponderable, indeterminate, caught in the endless web, the maze, the labyrinthine tangle of meaning.)[4]

Theory as we now know it, as the student guides have it, comprises, clearly, an awful lot of things. An awful lot; an aweful lot. Too many, you might readily think, for just one conceptual container; certainly too many for the minimalist pages of Jonathan Culler's *Literary Theory: A Very Short Introduction* (1999). Which is why Julian Wolfreys, for one, prefers Literary Theories. The great umbrella term 'Theory' is not only too convenient to be altogether true, it simplifies too much by its unhelpful homogenizing.

> However implicitly, 'literary theory' names a single point, rather than something composed, constructed or comprised of many aspects or multiple, often quite different identities. If we name several identities or objects as one, not only do we not respect the separateness or singularity of each of those subjects or identities, we also move in some measure towards erasing our comprehension of the difference between these objects and identities, making them in the process invisible.[5]

And that's well said (and like many other committed Theorists, Wolfreys is greatly distressed by any tendency to blunting the force of particular theoretical postures, deconstruction, feminism and so on, such as this homogenizing tendency represents). But still a kind of sense is served by this cramming-in label. For Theorists have indeed managed to pull off what is, by any standards, an astounding coup, or trick; have managed to wedge together a great many various subjects, concerns, directions, impulses, persuasions and activities that are going on in and around literature, and squeeze them all under the one large sheltering canopy of 'Theory'. They have managed to compel so many divergent wings of what they call Theory under the one roof, persuaded so many sectional variants of interpretative work to sink their possible differences around a common conference table, in the one seminar with the sign Theory on its door. So while setting

their faces, usually, against Grand Narratives and Keys to All Mythologies, as delusive and imperialist, and all that, Theorists have managed to erect the Grandest Narrative of all – Theory – the greatest
intellectual colonizer of all time. How this wheeze was pulled off,
how you can have the political and the personal subjects of literature – representations of selfhood and class and gender and race: the
outside-concerns, the outward look of writing, the descriptive and
documentary, the reformist intentions and the ideological instrumen-
tality of writing – envisioned and envisionable as absolutely part and
parcel of the often quite opposite and contradictory functions of writing – the merely formal, or the technically linguistic, or (as often) a
deeply inward, world-denying, aporetic writing activity – rather defies ordinary logic. Foundationalism and anti-foundationalism, shall
we say roughly the Marxist reading on the one hand, and the
deconstructionist on the other, make awkward bed-partners, you might
think. But Theory deftly marries them off, or at least has them more
or less cheerfully all registered as guests in the same hotel room.

The secret of these dangerous and strange liaisons, this hold-all
capaciousness of Theory, is, of course, embedded in the truly versatile
resources of Ferdinand de Saussure's *Cours de linguistique générale*, those
potent lectures given in Geneva to tiny handfuls of escapees from
nineteenth-century philology in the years up to and into the First
World War, and cobbled together later for posthumous publication
from students' notebooks. Saussure's wonderfully generous donation
to literary theory, and quite foundational for Theory's wide field of
interests, was a double-sided vision of linguisticity – on the one hand,
a radical menu of definitions of language as such, which fired and fed
concepts of signification as an activity on the inside only of language
and so also of text; on the other, a pointing to a new science of signs
in society, *semiotics*, a way of seeing and analysing all human structures
as like language, as in a deep way all textual. Here were the basics for
literary theory's so-called linguistic turn and the basis of Theory's obsessive linguisticity. The Saussurean terminology and concepts were
all set to be quite intellectually ravishing, and after the Second World
War when they spread to Western Europe and the Americas (they'd

19

mainly been taken up after the First World War in Eastern Europe) they became simply normative for literary study.

Saussure's brilliant suggestions caught on momentously. That language should be thought of as an affair of sign-systems rather than of words; that these systems were organized as sets of binaries – linked pairings of opposites – so that signs were binaries of *signifiant*, signifier (the written or spoken entity) and *signifié*, signified (the mental image produced by the sign); and the time and space of language, the language condition, were a binary of past and present, of the synchronic (language at any given moment) and the diachronic (language in history, the history of language); and language in existence was a binary of potential use and actual use (*langue* being the language *in potentia*, *parole* being language in action): all this became conventional wisdom, and a wisdom that quite ran away with Theory. Saussure said (correctly) that his binaries could not be separated in practice, but he chose in his lectures not to discuss signifieds or *parole* or diachrony. This was a mistake so far as his eager Theorizing followers would be concerned, for soon Theorists were saying, and thinking, that those aspects of language had been quite ruled out, didn't matter, and need not concern literary criticism. Reading literature did not need to take them into account, literature did not foreground them, being about signifiers rather than about signifieds, and not-historical (not of diachronic interest), and to do with *langue* rather than *parole*. These formalist preoccupations of Saussure-inspired Theory certainly sound now a bit crazy, a bit rich; but anyone who fails to credit them should glance at, say, Terence Hawkes's influential *Structuralism and Semiotics* (1977), a founding volume of the influential Methuen New Accents series of Theory paperbacks, and see them being cemented firmly in place for the student audience. It was all a cheeky traducing of Saussure, but a process furthered by more wrestings along the same misreading lines. Signs are arbitrary, said Saussure, and have little necessary link to what they denote – which has some truth in it: *cat* could easily be *dog*, to start with anyway – but quickly all of language, writing, meaning, were being declared to be arbitrary, not grounded in any reality, a mere illusion of language.

The 'arbitrariness of the signifier' – a non- Saussurean phrase, for him it was always the *arbitrariness of the sign* – set in as Theory's code for the linguistic life of literature, for literariness itself. Phonemes, the building blocks of words, comprised, according to Saussure, and again with truth, a system not of references but only of differences (*a* is not *b* is not *c*, and so on), but soon all linguistic and textual stuff was being thought of as differential rather than referential systems, cases of endless inward-looking deferrals of meaning, *mises en abyme* in the nice French coinage, writing plunging down for ever and ever into black holes of retreating signification. And soon Jacques Derrida was playing his astute game with the French word *différence*, to produce his coinage *différance*, so as to really bring home the deferral aspect of differential meaning, and to confirm his idea of the mere *jeu*, or play, or game of signifiers – a metaphor wrongly beefed up by his US mistranslators as the *freeplay* of signifiers, an idea not of Derrida's, but one soon found on hundreds of critical pages. And soon the old rhetorical term *aporia* was being brought into play – into *this* play – to point to the same claimed effect of uncatchable meaning – though *aporia* actually means a dead end, an end-stop, a cul-de-sac of sense-making, not its total disappearance down some linguistic black hole. And Jacques Lacan was quick to come up with talk of gaps and lacks, of *béances*, yawning holes of meaning – and soon every text possible was found to be full of those.

And, of course, this sequence of language–literature concepts was also getting itself applied to all the signifying practices out there in the world – the world of semiotics, of signs in society – as Saussure said they might. And soon everything was being seen as structured like a language, and language Saussureanly viewed. This was the high claim of Structuralism. The anthropologist Claude Lévi-Strauss became notable for reading, say, kinship structures as sets of Saussurean-type binaries. As revealed in tribal stories, these anthropological arrangements were of course linguistic and linguistified. Structural Anthropology was on its way. And Roland Barthes came to fame trying to read items of French culture (wrestling matches, and so on) as linguistic structures. His reading of French fashion magazines as a textualized system of the French fashion industry was more successful. But once started, this analytic furore need never stop its applications. The unconscious, for example, was also structured like a language, according to Jacques Lacan. And of course the structure was like a language on the Saussurean model as appropriated by literary Theorists – all signifiers and deferral. And Lacan, of course, produced his own 'algorithm' (he was fond of geometrical diagrams) for the current denigration of signifieds. The sign should be represented as $\frac{S}{s}$: big signifier over a very small signified, always sliding about deterringly and deferringly under the signifier that mattered more. And soon, such was the rapid circulation of such notions across the Theoretical stage, literary critics were burbling happily about sliding signifiers (see Colin McCabe, for instance, on their presence in Joyce, in his *James Joyce and the Revolution of the Word*, 1978). The linguistic trades defined the others, and the others returned to boost the literary. A glorious, amenable circularity of concept. A slippery sliding contagion.

Analogy-drawing is, of course, perennially worrying in the history of interpretations. 'Very like a whale', says old Polonius, too eagerly falling in with Hamlet's princely and mocking assertion that the clouds were so structured, and too happy to slide from his earlier ready assent that they were shaped like a camel, or backed like a weasel. Analogies are slippery customers and too-easy friends, and the language model came with all of the useful casual attractions of analogy. But catch on this one certainly did. In structuralist readings of literature, construing writing as built on phonemic or morphological sentence models, on binary lines, and so on – stimulated no end by the Saussure-stimulated Russian formalist Vladimir Propp and his *Morphology of the Folktale* (1928 in Russian, 1958 in English), a 'morphological' examination of a collection of Russian folktales. Which was all logical enough, because literature is made of language and if it won't submit to linguistic models, what will? But here was a set of language analogies applied also to everything that was made by the human language user. Everything, it was soon being alleged and grasped, could be seen and read on language lines, as textual, as text, or, as the concept held and fertilized, read as mere 'rhetoric', as 'discourse', as 'story', or 'narrative'.

The analytic brilliance of Michel Foucault was to extend the notion of 'discourse' across the whole globe of social constructs, but with particular fructifying force into his analysis of social areas where power operates to create social and individual subjugation, marginality, subalternity, in definitions of madness, illness, criminality, sexual deviance. The authoritarian arrangements of different periods, his arguments ran, were characterized by different 'discourses' or epistemic arrangements, i.e. are interpretable and comprehensible as rather like, if not always very like, a language or language stuff.[6] Foucault's inherited French leftism – and all the major French Theorists have been more or less, as they say, *Marxisant* – thus found new force as older views of class and economic oppression were rigorously re-spun as the gaze of oppressive authority, organized to mark the oppressed Other (prisoner, madman, schoolchild, the sick, the gay): this gaze a politicized version of Lacan's psychologized gaze; these Others a politicization of Lacan's otherness, with links to the old Saussurean/ new Derridean validation of difference. And how 'power' became an absolutely universal critical concept. And how the panoptic gaze of oppression – after Foucault's historical allegorization of the panopticon prisons of the nineteenth century in his *Surveillir et Punir* (1975), or *Discipline and Punish* (1977) – got everywhere. (The wised-up novelist Angela Carter even put a panopticon prison into the Russian section of her novel *Nights at the Circus*, 1984.) And, of course, this conceptual siding with the oppressed Other, with otherness, and with the socially different, readily linked hands with the analysis of *carnivalesque* by the exiled Russian Formalist Mikhail Mikhailovich Bakhtin in his *Rabelais and His World* (1968) – which in turn fell off the tree, so to say, into the lap of the Derridean idea of textuality as game. And Foucault's work not only had this power of drawing in its own analogies, but fed vividly back into the politicized analyses out of which (like carnivalesque) it had come. So that feminism, not least, so powerfully defined for older literary criticism by writers from Mary Wollstonecraft to Virginia Woolf, took on new life rearmed as it were by Foucault's gripping rhetorics of the discourses of power. And the other strong analytical -isms which are still potently with us as mainstays of Theory were also force-fed by Foucault's influential concepts:

studies such as postcolonialist ones, those angered investigations into imperialism fired originally by Marxism; and postcolonialism's twin, Black Studies, fired by equally angry analyses in the long aftermath of slavery, especially in the USA; and New Historicism, instigated by groups of old Marxists who were looking around in the wake of deconstruction for a legitimation of their literary–cultural historicist yearnings; and (so-called) Cultural Materialism, invented by one-time pure British Marxists and products of the powerful Cambridge (England) Raymond Williams–F. R. Leavis axis which spawned Terry Eagleton as well, namely Alan Sinfield and Jonathan Dollimore;[7] and, naturally, Queer Studies, utterly the godchild of Foucault's histories of sexuality. If Gender, Race and Class have become a dominant trinity of literary-critical concerns (as well as of Cultural Studies) – an unholy trinity according to the NAS and their kind – then it's Michel Foucault's work which brought them all brilliantly together (with the special emphasis, of course, on Gender and Race, especially in the USA, where Marxism has never been allowed to take strong root and class-consciousness and class rhetoric are by British and European standards deeply confused, and even taboo).

This linguistic–textual turn has succeeded in being a set of popular master tropes or keys, of course, by its canny inclusivity, its seemingly unstoppable adaptability, and obviously, its conceptual looseness. Henry Louis Gates, Jr, the most interesting of black spokesmen for American Black Studies, referring to the theory of literature which we all as reading individuals inevitably bring to our reading (our unwitting hybrid of theories), called it 'a critical gumbo as it were'.[8] *Gumbo*, from the Angolan *kingombo*, okra: the variously meat–fish–rice–okra stew of Cajuns and Creoles in Louisiana; name too for the hybrid French-based patois of Louisiana blacks and Creoles; label also for a kind of Cajun music mixing all kinds of sounds and styles. Gumbo is the essence of New Orleans and jazz, as Howard Mitcham has rhapsodically put it:

a mystique. . . . Like jazz and the blues, it has overtones of voodoo, mumbo-jumbo . . . tastes good . . . one-dish meal,

nourishing and filling . . . just sticks to your ribs . . . improvisa-
tional thing. . . . You just take off with whatever tune is handy,
and then you travel. You throw in a lot of blue notes, flatted
fifths, discords, and glissandos to spice it up, and the end result is
almost always satisfying. A Creole cook can take a handful of
chicken wings or a turkey carcass or a piece of sausage or a few
shrimps and crabs and whip up a gumbo. There are seafood
gumbos, chicken gumbos, wild duck and squirrel gumbos, meat
and sausage gumbos, okra and filé gumbos, and even a Lenten
gumbo called z'herbes, in which seven different types of gumbos
are used.[9]

Clearly gumbo is a lovely, multivalent, tasty (and slavery-derived,
postcolonial) mix that is most apt to Gates's postcolonial vision of the
American cultural *olla podrida*. Gates has rightly likened gumbo to the
ancient Roman *satura lanx*, the 'full plate' of mixed edibles, sweet or
sour, i.e. forced meat, farce-meat, stuffing, sausage-meat – what
Americanistically Gates calls 'hash' – which is one etymological root
of *satire*, and which traditionally helps define the rich mix of that genre
of writing.[10] Gumbo nicely captures the omnicomprehensiveness of
Theory in our textualizing era. Here, and like *this* – mainly unfarcically,
unsatirically, though with satirizable and farcical aspects – comes everything, potentially. And that's why Theory has spread so slickly, glibly
even, into so many domains of the humanities – into geography (the
surface of the earth is a text, and so are cities and weather systems and
so on);[11] and history (historiography is writing, ergo it's to be theorized as narrative and story and rhetoric, all tropologically, and its practitioners slotted into the gender, race and class boxes);[12] and music
(more textual product, subject to the squeeze, of course, of race and
class and gender; gender especially; can a flattened third be gay? why
yes indeed it can);[13] and theology (the Judaeo-Christian God and His
Book, all easily deconstructable and narrativizable; and as for patriarchy and logocentrism, why here are their foundations; deconstruction
begins, as it were, in the Book of Genesis);[14] and, of course, art
history(all texts);[15] and architectural theory and practice (all texts again,

25

and Daniel Libeskind deconstructs buildings!); and law (more text, and all deconstructable interpretative acts);[16] and medicine (the body is a text, after all).[17] Theory's gumbo-effect is why Cultural Studies, the study of anything and everything 'cultural', can claim coherence. Anything at all, in short, which can be thought of as if made textually, imagined as imagined, as narrated, as constructed language-like, and thus 'readable', is now being 'read'.

You do have to feel a bit sorry for the editors of the journal *Social Text*, so utterly taken in by Alan D. Sokal's spoof article 'Transgressing the Boundaries: Towards a Transformative Hermeneutics of Quantum Gravity', a very large bowl of Theory gumbo indeed. But Sokal moved in on quantum mathematics making all the right-sounding Theoretical anti-foundationalist and anti-hegemonic noises. 'Most recently, feminist and poststructuralist critiques have demystified the substantive content of mainstream Western scientific practice, revealing the ideology of dominance concealed behind the facade of "objectivity".' The assumptions of physics – 'that there exists an external world, whose properties are independent of any individual human being and indeed of humanity as a whole; that these properties are encoded in "eternal" physical laws; and that human beings can obtain reliable, albeit imperfect and tentative, knowledge of these laws by hewing to the "objective" procedures and epistemological strictures prescribed by the (so-called) scientific method' – are just, Sokal burbled merrily, one more set of post-Enlightenment dogmas to be busted with the tools of up-to-scratch Theory brought over from the literary–linguistic domain.[18] And why not? After all, the editors of *Social Text* had long ago come to believe in the universality of Theory's vision. And if geography and music and theology and the rest had succumbed to Theory, why not mathematics? Certainly, for Theorists, for Theory, all human pitches, and some non-human ones, have been as it were queered by the same analytical brush or brushes, and readily so. All of them 'constructed like a language'. And language, of course, sceptically regarded.

With Theory thus ecumenically conceived as being more or less all things to all women and men, offering something or other to more or less everyone of every gender and racial and class disposition and from every critical background, as some analytical touch or other for all textual occasions and seasons, the claim on the *necessity* of this or the other critical corner of Theory does indeed tend to dissolve into mere contingency, into questions of what's useful, or just handy, on any particular reading occasion. And of course handiness has been the key to Theory's success. Theory does open textual doors – with this key, if not quite that other one. The multiplying student guides mostly operate on this suck-it-and-see approach. You can have a go at 'reading like a woman', as it were, whoever you are; but then again, you might try a Marxized reading, or this week you can write me an essay using a New Historicist approach, and of course there's a stimulating Lacanianized article you might look at for the week after that. Douglas Tallack epitomizes this Theoretical pragmatism, or opportunism, very nicely with his volume *Literary Theory at Work* (1989), in which the Nottingham University Theory Group run various Theoretical approaches, from narratological through political to deconstructive and psychoanalytic, across three texts, Conrad's *Heart of Darkness*, Henry James's *In the Cage* and D. H. Lawrence's *St Mawr*. And they all compel, more or less.[19]

'Which Theory?' asks Raman Selden in the introduction to his *Practising Theory and Reading Literature: An Introduction*, and he means which Theory for me, for you, in this or any other reading situation. And the answer is a '*de facto* pluralism'. 'It may seem best to say "Let many flowers bloom" and to treat the plenitude of Theories as a cornucopia to be enjoyed and tasted with relish.' Or dip into your gumbo, as you wish, in your own time. Selden disowns a 'market economy' approach, he says, but that is what his approach to Theory's multiplex of approaches suggests: shop around; roll your own; pick'n'mix (excluding, it always goes without saying, a racist, male-chauvinist, fascistic, master-class approach). This liberalism is for many analysts the very essence of 'postmodernity'. It is, precisely, where Theory has arrived with its espousal of multivalence and multiculturalism and its suspicions of canons, and evaluation, and, in effect, truth-claims. It is, though, an eclecticism which naturally vexes many purists, who do survive among Theorists, for the various sections of Theory thus plundered often started out as very rigid kinds of analysis, steeped in the particulars of their ideological sources. Such and such are how language and the self really are, say Saussure and Freud and Marx and Lacan and Derrida and all the rest of the prophetic tribe, and so this and this is how writing and text actually are. And many Theorists, the really devout believers and ideologues, essentially claim that you should, you must, read like a deconstructionist, or a woman, or a lesbian, or a slave-emancipationist; for if you do not you are untrue to the nature of things, and of language, are obtuse and myopic about history and repression, and so on. Only thus and thus might criticism live up to the criticism implicit in its name.

The 'domestication' of Theory evidenced by the handbooks and liberal university courses is just what worries Julian Wolfreys, for example – a good case of the Theorist who wants Theory to retain a radicalism of critique. The Theory Course acts, he complains, like a set of rabies shots; it's a quarantining effect; 'an effective form of containment' working by a false flattening out and homogenizing. It's a sort of mere Theory tourism ('If this is week six it must be feminism').[20] But Wolfreys's own volume simply joins the long roster of guides ministering to this tourism effect. It props up the assumption of Theory as a mere self-service counter; sustains the cheerful pragmatism of Richard Rorty, for whom all hard-and-fast rules of reading are simply misguided (the 'view that "theory" – when defined as an "attempt to govern interpretations of particular texts by appealing to an account of interpretation in general" – has got to go').[21]

The Old Bolsheviks, as we might call them, the true Theoretical believers, prize what they believe to be the absolute revolutionary force of the linguistic turn, especially in its high deconstructive mode. And many European Theorists, and not just the French, as well as some North Americans and lots of South Americans, did indeed start out as Old Leftists, committed to a basic notion of literary-critical hermeneutic truth as nothing if not revolutionary, as the ultimate turnaround. They found it easy, even necessary, to talk of absolute losses of old critical currencies, total disruptions of old positions by new ones, a 'split in the psyche of traditional literary studies', a 'true break' with, say, 'the Romantic inheritance', and so on. (I take all of these firm *coupure*/cut/break terms almost randomly from Raman Selden's introduction to his *Practising Theory and Reading Literature*.) Catherine Belsey – an Old Bolshevik of Theory if ever there was one – reminds us in her feistily dogmatic *Critical Practice* (1980) that Freud liked to think he'd made a Copernican revolution by unsettling old ideas of selfhood, and Lacan agreed with him. Belsey, though, devotes the last part of her book to arguing that it was Lacan's Saussureanized continuation of Freud's decentring of the self that was truly Copernican. These revolutionary dreams are characteristic of our Theorists. But, in truth, there is nothing in Theory which has proved utterly revolutionary – all of it being, manifestly, new spins on old turns, a continuing affair of what T. S. Eliot in his 1930 conversion poem *Ash Wednesday* dubbed a turning and turning again.

In many ways there is only one history of literary theory – and wiser counsels increasingly realize it – as witnessed neatly in Chadwyk-Healey's 2001 *Literary Theory* database: 'which traces literary theory and criticism from Plato to the present day', or from Aristotle to Derrida, as their publicity has it. Certainly everything that Theory comprises, operates in one zone or another, or in some combination, of what have proved the main continuing focuses of literary theory since poetics and discussion of aesthetics began with the Greeks and Romans. There's only ever been up for critical grabs, for theory, a simple trio of knowable, thinkable, zones, corresponding to the three components of the basic model of linguistic communication. There is always, and only ever, a sender, a message, and a receiver – a writer, a text, a reader – the act of writing, the thing written, the reading of the written thing – the literary input, the literary object found to be 'there', reader(s) attending to this thereness. Or, if you like: cause, consequence, effect. Only three; but a mighty three for all that. And the whole history of criticism, of theorizing, is merely a history of the varying, shifting preoccupation across the ages with these three zones, and with these three alone. These three, and only these three, define the range, the nature, of literary theorizing. It's what's done with them, the varying emphases and definitions which they have received

29

over time, that defines the history, as it defines the politics, of theorizing.

Rarely has past critical fashion chosen to emphasize all three simultaneously. Critical fashion has always been notably picky and partial. The busy co-presence of all three in Theory is one sign of the ways modern or postmodern theory is spun differently from the theorizing of the past: it's a marker of the greedy omnivalence of Theory's gumbo. But however partially or fully dwelt on in the theorizing of a given historical moment, these three – their avatars, their rejiggings and redefinings, their formulations and reformulations, their various turns and returns – are always the three, from the beginning to now, from theoretic Genesis to modern Theoretical Apocalypse, or (in those lovely words in *Finnegans Wake*) from guinesses to apolkaloops.

Only the temporary emphasis and focus shift – as a sketchy sketch map of the last two-and-a-half millennia of literary theory readily shows. Plato is preoccupied with what poetry says, its untruth, and so with its negative moral effect on audiences. Authors only feature in Plato's *Republic* as venal persons to be banished for perpetrating immorality. For his part, Aristotle concentrates on the form and nature of the text (tragedy, he says in his *Poetics*, is the imitation of an action, it has a beginning, middle and end, its subject is constrained by the unities of time and place, and so on), and he's greatly interested in emotional and ethical effects on audiences, their *katharsis*. He implies much about authors and the act of writing, but says little or nothing about these. For his part, Horace's greater concern is with literature's operations on readers and audiences, the twin combination of the *utile* and *dulce* of texts, their pleasurable moral instructiveness. And Longinus also stressed the results of literature – uplift, sublimity. And when the Renaissance rediscovers these theorists it plugs these emphases hardest. Philip Sidney's *Defence of*, or *Apology for*, *Poetry* (1595) discusses content and effect intensely and lyrically (does the poet lie? no, because he 'nothing affirmeth'; poetry's sweet kathartic purging is a 'medicine of cherries'; moral effect through emotional effect is good particularly for men, tyrants, soldiers, horsemen; and so on), but Sidney is utterly relaxed, along with his classical sources, about writers and the act of writing. Rather differently, Edmund Spenser's anxiety to make a great national epic is as much to do with what the poet manages with his linguistic materials as with his Protestant nationalism's moral and political effect on readers, and *The Faerie Queene* is a great language experiment (inspired by the programme for reforming the poetic language developed by Boileau and the French Pléiade movement).[22]

The neo-classicists were for their part keenest on theorizing the work of writing on and for audiences. For John Dryden poetry defines a nation: Shakespeare is the centre of a national poetry; tragicomedy, an English invention, puts French writers and above all French critics, in their place; the triumph of Shakespeare, the nation's Bard, is analogous to, as it is contemporaneous with, military victory – with the naval defeat of the Dutch, for example, by ships whose cannon can be heard firing in the English Channel even as Dryden's theorists assemble for their critical symposium on Dramatic Poesy.[23] For his part Dr Johnson is rightly renowned for his great Christian interest in the moral effects of writing. His criticism, like that of his contemporaries Dryden and Swift and Pope, is the work of a great literary satirist, and like theirs is linked to the moral and political reformist intents of the satirist. Johnson's moral preoccupations are given force by his extraordinarily intense emotional engagements with texts. He theorizes as an extremely emotional reader. He simply cannot bear to read about the Fall in Milton's *Paradise Lost* because the Judaeo-Christian story of the genesis of sinfulness and loss of innocence is too distressing to dwell on; the blinding of Gloucester and the death of Cordelia make *King Lear* truly unabidable.[24] Johnson's theoretical emphasis on the reading result is entirely geared by this personal emotionality in response to writings. But he is also an editor (in a great age of editors; at the heart of a time that was seeking, especially, to make sense of and to establish the texts of Shakespeare). He's also a lexicographer, in a great age of dictionary-makers, so his textual concerns are intensely alert, as never before, to the problems of the etymologies and semantics of vernacular writing.[25] And with his *Lives of the Poets* (1783) Johnson also becomes the theorist–critic who really started literary biography off in English. For the first time English criticism took the writer, the writing life of the producer of literature, seriously as a factor in the writing product. Not surprisingly, Johnson's admirer James Boswell's *Life of Johnson* (1791) became our first extended writer's life – the model which launched a thousand emulators.

Biography is, of course, a great Romantic mode. And Johnson and Boswell are classicists becoming Romantics. Typically, for Blake, Milton's importance is as the man in the poem. And for the Romantics the literary axis which mattered was the contract, the communion, between the man in the poem and the poem's reader. Wordsworth's great preface to the second edition of *Lyrical Ballads* (1800) is all about how poets get their inspiration from emotional experience out in nature, relive it in their verses, and so pass it on to their readers. Out of authorial sublimity, a readerly sublime. Notoriously – even if the conventional judgement is a harsh one – the Romantics valued the mere fact of being inspired (the poet as Coleridge's Aeolian harp, or Shelley's glowing coal, receiving the winds of an uncovenantable inspiration to produce poetic music and poetic fire), more than what was actually written under the spirit's guidance. And this leaving texts as it were to take care of themselves or, more importantly, to theorize themselves, continues to this day in the more vatic quarters of literary production – which doesn't mean that Yeats, say, who really believed in spirit guides and automatic writing, or D. H. Lawrence, who enters eagerly into the ranting tradition of his Nonconformist forebears, did not also, at times anyway, most carefully revise their work. Though, observably (and this again is conventional wisdom) Romantic poets commonly tinker with the first 'inspired' efforts to the detriment of their texts; and they do, like Coleridge, or D. H. Lawrence, seem often unable to stop writing and talking when the spirit is moving, and just stop dead when the spirit leaves them (think of Coleridge's *Kubla Khan*), and they prefer starting all over again to revising (the several versions of Lawrence's *The Lost Girl* and *Lady Chatterley's Lover* are good examples).

But the theory position remains always one of emphasis and concentration on one or other of the Big Three rather than absolute neglect, and the 'progress' of criticism and theory sticks at being a game with only three dimensions. So it went, and so it still goes. The great nineteenth-century critic Thomas Carlyle is, of course, immersed in textualities (his zany *Sartor Resartus* (1836) is as dotty on wild textuality as anything promoted by *Tristram Shandy* or *Shandy*'s postmodern admirers), but he's also a post-Romantic literary biographer and keen to promote poets as heroes of the age. Matthew Arnold, too, is interested in authors, and talks amply about text ('the best' that's been 'thought and said'), but like most Victorians his main preoccupation is with poetry's moral and social effects. For Arnold, poetry is an acculturating mechanism. It educates and socializes. Above all, it consoles and instructs readers as a secular substitute for the instructions and consolations once provided by the texts and readings of the now challenged Christian religion. But the theoretical emphasis had switched away from the romantic stress on the poet as the main thing, and was now directed very much towards the reader, the context, the world, and bore strongly on personal, and so also on social construction, on up-building, or (to use the older and Christian term) edification. And that was as true of George Eliot as it was of Marx and those great Victorian survivors and inspirees, T. S. Eliot and F. R. Leavis.

Other emergers from the nineteenth century went in for reaction and reemphasis rather than affirmation, of course. What made Ferdinand de Saussure open his *Cours* with a lengthy discussion of linguisticity as such was precisely a reaction against the nineteenth-century concentration on philology, on language in history, in the world outside of language (he was after all a Professor of Sanskrit). Saussure might even be thought of as catching the spirit of the late-nineteenth-century reaction away from realism and towards symbolism, aestheticism, formalism, imagism, and the text burning with a hard gem-like flame purely and uncontaminated by the world. And the Russian Formalists Saussure inspired in his turn were steeped in that same reactionary spirit – which is why Formalism soon fell foul of the new Soviet regime which looked back with yearning on the nineteenth-century theorists' preoccupation with the work's dynamic relation to the context, out there where the readers were, as the source

33

of all aesthetic good – which was a reaction against the modernist reaction: truly reactionary, as one might say. And, after all, the founders of Marxist aesthetics, Marx and Engels, were nothing if not High Victorians. And this quarrel between the formalizers and the politicizers became one of the twentieth century's recurrent causes of theoretical warfares. I. A. Richards, inventor of Practical Criticism, and his theoretical offspring the Chicago New Critics, vigorously resisted the politicizing and theologizing of reading that went on in the 1920s and 1930s hand in glove with Soviet doctrinism and/or its Fascist and Christian antagonists. The 'verbal ikon' was the only thing for the New Critics, the text as a self-subsistent 'well-wrought urn', with all other critical preoccupations and emphases ruled sharply out as heresies.

Structuralism, and then deconstruction, descended more or less straight out of Saussure's formalism, with much theoretical support from the particular stress granted to the amazing narrative and rhetorical structures of the 'dream text' by Saussure's great contemporary Sigmund Freud. Freud did, naturally, have real patients and their therapy in mind, real selves producing the dream texts whose interpretation would, *hoffentlich*, lead to actual cures. And so, arguably, did Jacques Lacan. But as Freud's work tended to get appropriated as a set of clues to mere textual penetration (Hamlet's problem 'is' the Oedipus complex), so Lacan's most notable contribution to literary theory has been on the merely textual front (sliding signifiers; textual *baiences*; and so forth); which has not stopped him also reinforcing the politicizers with their discourses of 'the other'. But then Saussurean difference has also been able to take on a political edge at the politicizers' behest; and Michel Foucault, the great inspirer of New Historicism and the rest, drew happily and profitably on such originally formalist notions to reinvigorate his own Marxism. Which brings us back, of course, to Theoretical gumbo, as well as potently illustrating the point about theoretical revision being more the norm than theoretical revolution.

Criticism always claims newness; it wants to be new. It's not just writers who want (as Ezra Pound put it) to 'make it new'. But criticism has never ever been quite new; and the history we're dealing with is all about swings and roundabouts, about the Big Three items going around and coming around, again and again, in a process of constant reaction, resurrection, rereading, repositioning, revision. Aristotle overturns Plato; Sidney takes on his Puritan contemporaries armed with polished-up Aristotelian tools; the formalists resist the realists who in turn object to formalism; Lacan rereads Freud; Althusser rereads Marx; Leavis wars with the New Critics, who fight the Marxists; Derrida moves away from Marxism and is repudiated by Foucault; Derrida reclaims the self and history and 'presence' from his deconstructionist fans who reject those things in his name (and is welcomed back into the fold by Foucault). And so on, systole and diastole, fading and returning, on and on.

Revisionism is, of course, always striated with nostalgia. Soviet Socialist Realism, for example, wanted a simple nineteenth-century realism to return to displace rampant modernism and formalism. And our modern Theory has, more than any previous set of theoretical notions and practices, provoked in its adversaries the wish to reinstate some earlier period's theory and to return to a mythic period of greater theoretical or cultural purity before multiculturalism (or 'multi-culti' with its deliberately pejorative ring of *cult* in it) arrived to derange what's thought of as an earlier homogeneity of language and disposition (a kind of aestheticized racism, this), before deconstruction (rhymes with destruction, of course, in its detractors' ears), before the 'culture of complaint', as it's been dubbed, set in and whingeing feminists or black-studies students got loud. But no simple return to prelapsarian theoretical innocence is ever possible, for that never existed. There never was such a theory arcadia as Theory's opponents allege. The offensive concerns of Theory have always been present in some form or another, muted often, differently loaded frequently, but still there. Theory has always been fallen, as it were. What worries some, and excites others, about our recent Theory is by no means its innovativeness, but only what are in effect its strong renovations.

There certainly is strong renovation. Theoretical rereading is indeed rereading. Marx is Foucauldianized. Freud is indeed Lacanianized. The formalizings of old New Criticism get more forcefully reinstated as Structuralism. The 'biographical fallacy' of the New Critics reappears more extremely as Barthes's Death of the Author. Russian Formalism feeds, in a real sense, into deconstruction, but more intensely. Old Historicism segues into New Historicism, but it's a historicism with grave doubts about history. And, of course, there is, and will be, inevitable revisionism of Theory's pushes. The intensity of the politicization of criticism was in many ways a reaction to the strength with which deconstruction's anti-foundationalism took hold. A once derided Humanism has rearrived as the Anthropological Turn.[26] If anything, literary biography intensified as a critical activity, especially in England, in the wake of Roland Barthes's declaration of the death of the author. And proceeding critically by rethinking genre and the generic gets revived. And emotionality returns to the fore, again.[27] And Johnson's religious moralism keeps returning – as Coleridge's or Arnold's or T. S. Eliot's or Leavis's – and is an old influenza then caught (yes, really) by Gender and Race studies as well as by the Class preoccupations in which it got caught up among the Victorians.

What deceives both those shocked, as well as those besotted by Theory, is that the returners, whether welcomed or despised, never wear exactly the same hat they wore to go away in. Raymond Williams once famously claimed, in an echo of Milton's vexed assertion in his *Areopagitica*, that 'new presbyter' was 'but old priest writ large', that new structuralism was but old New Criticism writ large. And he was right, but not quite right. The theoretical return is always contaminated by what went on meanwhile. Althusser is Marx put through the Saussurean wringer. Lacan sharply Saussureanizes Freud. New historicism is by no means a simple reprise of old historicism, but historicizing inevitably affected by the historically intervening supremacy of textuality, so that its founding guru Stephen Greenblatt, though recognizably still a Marxist of sorts, is one whose model of the historical input and output of writing is greatly complicated by an interest in the input rather of texts into texts, and in texts' output rather as textual (a 'circulation of texts', as it's called, replacing other kinds of circulation – say of persons and things, materialities, into texts and out again into the world of persons and things). And twentieth-century Socialist Realism is far more narrow and exclusive than nineteenth-century social realism. And the Death of the Author concept is indeed several steps more murderous than the Biographical Fallacy – which never imagined a dead author, only one critics shouldn't talk about. And when the 'new' biography sets in it is infected by the new gender issues, and foregrounds issues of hermeneutics, and expresses doubts about the authority of its stories in a metatextual way owing everything to Theory. The self-reflexiveness of Peter Ackroyd's *Dickens* and the canny anti-biography which is Richard Holmes's *Dr Johnson and Mr Savage* are classics, almost, of self-conscious post-Theory biography.[28] And when the question of reader emotionality returns as a critical concern, though it will usually involve some discussion of Aristotelian katharsis, or pause over the Johnsonian repertoire of highly charged textual encounters, it is also differently inflected from all its earlier occasion – whether in, say, I. A. Richards's rejection of emotional response as a criterion of value in 1920s Cambridge, or in Wolfgang Iser's interest in readers' responses, or in the weight given to questions of emotion in the Canon Wars provoked by our Gender, Race and Class debates. The returns of Theory are inevitably incremented.

For all that, theorizing about literature is always a palimpsest. Below the latest lines you can always still read the older inscribings. Theoretical memory is always stronger than Theory's would-be revolutionaries hope. The present trend of Theory is always a simultaneously present archeology or paleography. Theory's archive is perpetually open. As with the media of communication. We move from script to print to IT, but I still start writing this with a pen and pencil. Now I fly, now I drive my car, now I ride my bike, now I go on foot. While Concorde flies supersonically overhead, a canal barge goes by and a railway train, and, as Larkin has it in his poem 'The Whitsun Weddings', there's always someone 'running up to bowl'.

In denying Theory's absolute innovativeness, I'm seeking to place it rather than simply denigrate it. And, to be sure, if Derrida and Foucault are, as it were, Theory's Concorde – if, for that matter, our Theory gumbo is like flying Jumbo – then it's easy to believe the excitement that Theory's turns and turnabouts have generated. And in truth, there has been, and there is the good, and the goods, of Theory.

4

The Good of Theory

Yet we do not doubt that at the heart of this immense volubility,
this flood and foam of language, this irreticence and vulgarity
and triviality, there lies the heat of some great passion. . . . It
should be our delight to watch this turmoil, to do battle with the
ideas and visions of our own time, to seize what we can use, to
kill what we consider worthless, and above all to realize that we
must be generous to the people who are giving shape as best
they can to the ideas within them.

Virginia Woolf, 'Hours in a Library'

The incremented returns of Theory have indeed borne increments of
critical value. There is no doubt in my mind that Theory has really
revitalized the study of literature since the Second World War. Anyone who was a student in the early 1960s (like me) will recall the
sheer dullness of the by-then established New Critical routines suffo-
cating reading in their affectionate but strangulating grip, and the sinking
feeling that a future in criticism might actually mean a whole lifetime
of reading (and writing) yet one more minute clarification of some
line or lines for *The Explicator*, and that's all. Some blend of Marxism
and F. R. Leavis – Raymond Williams, in fact, as I recall – came as a
blessed relief. And when news of the great linguistic turn started to
roll in, in the later 1960s, it was an even greater alleviating turnaround
– especially when it proved a textual gumbo you could stir whole
dollops of politicizing and moralizing back into. (I remember the excitement of first hearing of Roland Barthes and opening his *Writing*

Degree Zero: it was like my earlier introduction to Beckett's *Watt* – like being Keats in the poem about first looking into Chapman's Homer.)

In many respects, reading is so much more alive under the impact of Theory than it was; texts have in many ways become so much more vividly present, so much richer and deeper, in their newly acquired valencies. John Bunyan thought Mr Facing-Both-Ways a bad thing, and wandering into Bypath Meadow a dangerous temptation to Christians, because true pilgrims should look and go in only one heavenward direction, be unflinchingly monovisual, and remain all undistracted. And Bunyan was, of course, an admirably plain-sense-only-of-scripture man. But Theory has massively enriched reading by precisely inducing readers to pursue its multi-directional potentialities, to relish the gumbo. We're all Mr and Mrs Facing-All-Ways nowadays. The reading agenda has been massively bulked out, both in terms of what is read under the banner of English or Literature, and also in terms of the critical dispositions the reader is invited by Theory to adopt. Canons of what to read and how, have not just 'fallen', as the poet John Ashbery once put it, but they have been bulked out extraordinarily.

The great good of deconstruction has been to make readers all at once uneasy about easy meanings, and relaxed about polyphony, multiplicity, puzzle, and meaning over-spill. The view of reading that celebrates textual play for its own sake – the *jeu des signifiants* (play, not freeplay, that misleading mistranslation), kicking the ball around the hermeneutic park for the sheer joy of it, as preached up by Jacques Derrida in his Two Interpretations of Interpretation lecture, has relaxed criticism for its own good. A theoretical thrust which brings the playful *Tristram Shandy* and its Shandyesque postmodernist offspring in from a Johnson–Leavis sponsored outer darkness ('Nothing odd will do long; *Tristram Shandy* did not last': Dr Johnson) is obviously gainful.[1] Suspecting quick and ready outcomes from the reading squeeze on a text has made many readers not only gamier but cannier. The traditional idea that you will know more or less precisely where you 'come out' (that nice Henry James metaphor) at the end of a poem or play or novel – blessed, enlightened, purged, greatly aware of what's been acquired in knowledge as well as experience, leaving the page or the theatre, as classically at the end of Milton's *Samson Agonistes*, 'with new acquist / Of true experience from this great event / With peace and consolation . . . / And calm of mind all passion spent' – has been well challenged, and unsettled, if not actually unseated. Critics from Aristotle to Freud had wrestled for centuries with the paradox of the pleasurable pain resulting from serious art (the question Anthony Nuttall deftly encapsulated in 1996 as *Why Does Tragedy Give Pleasure?*). But the idea that pleasure at the end should include a complacent sense of knowing well and truly what the poem, or whatever, truly means is a pleasure principle too far. The 'hermeneutics of suspicion' eagerly inculcated by deconstruction is far truer to the reinterpretable nature of serious and classic writings – one thinks of the constant rereadings of the Bible and Virgil and Dante and Shakespeare and so on and on, of the way *Hamlet*, say, keeps yielding meaning but also seems to keep withholding it – retaining, like its hero, the 'mystery' which inter-preters keep on trying to 'pluck out' (*Hamlet*, III.ii.354-ish). *Aporia*, that favourite rhetorical device or position which deconstructive read-ings keep uncovering, when the quest for meaning seems to have got stuck in a labyrinth of possibilities, trapped in uncertainties, faced with the forking paths of several significations, at some sort of dead end, at the abysmal bottomlessness of the text's dark culs-de-sac, down in the arsehole of the textual bag (not to be confused with J. R. R. Tolkien's jollier Hobbit-hole Bag End), has, of course, been well recognized for centuries. 'Aporia is a figure whereby the speaker sheweth that he doubteth, either where to begin for the multitude of matters, or what to do or say in some strange or ambiguous thing', is how John Smith defined *aporia* in 1657 in *The Mysterie of Rhetorique Unveil'd*. George Puttenham, the great translator of Greek and Latin rhetorical terms into English in his *Arte of English Poesie* (1589: for women, he said, people unschooled in ancient languages), glossed *aporia* as 'the Doubtfull'. And so deconstruction's stressing of doubt as a normal consequence of reading restores a well-canvassed ancient sense of fre-quent defeat before (and after) the text. Which is true, not least, to that recurring reader-feeling of puzzlement even after protracted wrestlings with a text, and the occasional suspicion that maybe it's the text's fault and not mine that I can't tell just what it means. This coincides too with many an author's confession that try as they might they couldn't quite say what they wanted to. (Iris Murdoch, for example, charged with the way her novels did not live up to the criteria of her critical writings would just shrug and say that that was how it turned out. And what, after all, are an author's revisions, those sometimes endless tinkerings with the words on the page, a sign of, than a dissatisfaction over not 'getting it right' first – or second, or third – time, or ever?) It fits, too, with the common-or-garden speaker's annoyance or apology over not being 'able to put it into words'. 'That is not what I meant at all. That is not it at all' – as T. S. Eliot's Prufrock imagines a woman saying to him. The linguistic turn is to be credited with leaving all of us bereft of linguistic and hermeneutic complacency.

And if Theory has opened, or reopened, our eyes to textual irresolution, stickiness, awkwardness, it has certainly opened many eyes to meanings in texts previously quite unregistered or only dimly perceived. The great texts, the canonical works of the old literature syllabuses – Shakespeare, and his contemporaries, Milton, the Romantic poets, Jane Austen, the great Victorian poets and novelists, and so forth – have not only been fruitfully mined for their deconstructive refusals of meaning, their lacks and gaps and *aporias* and busy plunges into abysmal significations and signifying abysms, but also for presences formerly unnoticed or disregarded and rightly regarded now as always important and often absolutely central to a work's meanings – particularly, of course, women, blacks, gays, subaltern persons, repressed groups, minorities, the edge-out and disempowered. True, before the Theory explosion an older feminism had started acknowledging women as literary subject and object; and British Marxists had from the 1920s on begun seriously attending to working-class writers and voices; and Irish and Commonwealth studies had more latterly begun attending to the colonized writer and subject previously occluded within the generic label 'English Literature'. But now such

41

once ignored and unrecognized presences – the formerly 'mute in-
glorious Jane Austens', as Virginia Woolf labelled them in *A Room of
One's Own* (1929) – are a norm of reading interest. How could we –
at least how could the practitioners in the old critical centres and
establishments – miss, we now wonder, Henry Fielding's novelist sister Sarah, or Fanny Burney, or manage to pay no attention to the
colonial sources of Jane Eyre's money, and the black-creole face of
Bertha Mason, the Mad Woman in *Jane Eyre*'s attic; or discuss the
encounter in Dickens's *Dombey and Son* of wealthy Mr Dombey and
his friend Joey Bagstock with Mr Toodles the soot-caked stoker on
the London–Birmingham train, a meeting much analysed by Marxists
and Leavisites, without pondering the silent presence on the railway
platform of Bagstock's Indian servant, 'the Native'? How could we
not take into account the force of homosexuality in the fictions and
criticism of Gide and Wilde and Auden and . . . and . . .; or not notice
how far writing is so totally taken up with the body that it is from end
to end a great somatic stunt, a theatre of bodies on display, a battlefield
of the wounded, mutilated and dying, an anatomy theatre, a great
dissecting table of the cut-open, probed, tented, haruspicated corpse?
How were we able to prattle on about Caliban without thinking about
the institution of slavery, or, for that matter, rest content with white
actors blacking up to play Othello? How could we? That we do so no
longer is a tribute to Theory. 'Is there a woman in this text?' we ask
now as normally, and very properly, as once we asked whether there
was an irony or an ending, a moral revelation or a Christ-figure. By
the same token, we wonder without any sense of forcing about the
presence, or indeed the significant absence of, or silence about, blacks,
and gays, and 'signifying monkeys', and subalterns, and bodies, of all
kinds and types. Our textual communities and cities and lands are so
much more vividly peopled, so much more amply presenced, now
than before Theory.

And it's not just that reading Shakespeare or Dickens is, to put it at
its simplest, so much more interesting now, a matter of so much
absorbingly thicker detail in the text, than before. But whole chronological periods of writing, whole genres, whole literary areas, have

been revitalized by Theory-induced rereads. The Elizabethan period, for example, is now quite incandescent with Foucauldianized life – all a matter of power and body theatricalized, on display, a scene ravaged by the dialectics, the tensions, the horrors of the crimes and plagues and brothels of Elizabethan London, especially down on the South Bank of the Thames, to which Foucault-inspired readings have directed our newly attentive gaze, where the theatres and the stews and the plague-houses jostled side by side. The new Theorized readings have been like the switching on of a bright light. And the same goes for Augustan London and its writing, a place now of more vivid tension than ever between posh Whitehall and Grub Street, along a Thames more awash than ever with dead dogs and Smithfield excrements; or for Dickensian London, where great fortunes jangle against ruinous slums and fine ladies paddle in horse-shit now much more vividly than ever they did. We knew of these literary places before, but Theory has made them so much more luminous. They're truly *im Licht*, all in a new light, like Berlin lit up in the Weimar period, *Berlin im Licht*, to reveal the gargoyle undergrowths and grim truths, the criminalities and darknesses, all the repressed stuff brought potently into vision as never before. And these are places – *sites* as the Theory jargon has it – not just as places where literature was produced and so places whose awful and aweful realities are reflected in writing, but places made knowable precisely in their literary forms, as *literatured*, to use Joyce's term from *Finnegans Wake*. For what Theory has really brought home is the utterly main function of literature as a shaper of the realities we perceive – of Elizabethan London, or colonialism, or the black, the gay, the female, and so on, as 'constructed' for us by the texts we know them through, the 'discourses' which make up our personal vision, ideology, sense of things, and are main features of the large 'discourse', or *episteme* (to use another of Foucault's fundamental terms), of our, or any, 'time'. Theory's sense of literature's agency – its role in the active production of social and political meanings – is a major contribution to a notion of what poeticity is, of what literature is 'for'. Too, Theory's refusal to allow this great imaginative work of writing – its great help in building up our whole *imaginaire*, our imaginative repertoire, our grasp of the things we know and the ways we know them – any political neutrality, or innocence, has been very bracing indeed for criticism. If the old Arnold–Leavis vision of writing's moral effect granted writing and the reading effort terrific importance, Theory's more recent sense of writing as a key part of the social and political constructive work of 'discourse' only increases those feelings of literary importance and so also of critical obligation.

And the scope of these realizations is so much the more ample than once it might have been because of the great extensions of the literary syllabus, the literary canon or canons, which Theory's interests have brought about. On every hand the range of the (academically) readable has increased. In large terms, Theory defies the narrow syllabus, the list of the readable and studiable drawn up on narrow criteria, especially on some (now) patently obvious ideological basis, so that only men's or white people's or Europeans' or Christians' works get in, or predominate. Theory has meant highly successful challenges to the idea of Great Books courses consisting only of DWEMs, those much deplored Dead White European Males. Theory challenges the idea of sparse Great Traditions, or even of Great Traditions at all. F. R. Leavis is a usual target for his limiting of quality in the English novel to a small elite of Austen, George Eliot, James Conrad and Lawrence, and dismissing the 'ruck' of Gaskells and Trollopes, as he put it, and calling Charlotte Brontë minor, and jeering at *Moll Flanders* and Virginia Woolf and *Tristram Shandy*, and only allowing in *Hard Times* out of all Dickens's novels.[2]

Some over-elated Theorists have dismissed the very idea of canons and canonical lists. And of course, as crudely put – Top Tens, Top Hundreds, Essential Reading – they do sound crude. Writing and writers should not be made at all to resemble footballers or movies or music albums. But the real argument is not about crass elitisms, nor even about a democracy of writers and readers, but reflects the charge that canons are always ideological constructs. It draws strongly on a poststructuralist allegation that hierarchies are always there to be deconstructed – even if they are not actually, as some people believe, automatically self-deconstructing, self-inverting entities. Theorists have preferred working busily to topple Big Names from off their special canonical pedestals. Shakespeare's usual lofty rating has caused particular resentment to canon-busters, and a whole critical industry has built up to expose his topmost position and Bardolatry and the Shakespeare publishing and theatrical industries as a sham and a fraud, as well as a key illustration of the real emptiness and mere nationalist and/or commercial manipulation that makes any and every canon. And Gary Taylor's *Reinventing Shakespeare: A Cultural History from the Restoration to the Present* (1990) makes especially interesting reading along these lines. (It doesn't altogether convince me, and it and its ilk will not, I guess, succeed in really toppling Shakespeare, whose merits and strengths and depths and widths have been, and are, clear to most readers and do not need the strong counter-advocacy of, say, Jonathan Bate's *The Genius of Shakespeare* (1997), or Harold Bloom's *The Western Canon: The Books and School of the Ages* (1994) or his *How to Read and Why* (2000), let alone his *Shakespeare: The Invention of the Human* (1999), to prop them up.)

The Shakespeare palaver is extreme, even if it is undoubtedly representative of the sharper edge of DWEM hostilities and the wilder intents of some canon-warriors (and there are indeed attempts in Britain to shove him off lists of compulsory texts for school examinations in English Literature; and the NAS does report that studying Shakespeare was compulsory in only 16 per cent of the US English departments it surveyed in 1997–8, compared with 48 per cent in 1964–5). But by and large canon-busting has done great good – most good, in fact – in bursting open the syllabus doors to authors travelling in one-time out-group categories, such as black, Afro-American, colonial, female, gay, popular, low, sentimental, or even patently deconstructive or postmodernist.[3] The all-out-top living author studied in the USA, according to the NAS, is the Nobel Prize winning Afro-American woman Toni Morrison, with Alice Walker, another distinguished female Afro-American, coming in second. The top male, Salman Rushdie, came fourth in the NAS survey – and, pertinently, he's a postcolonial East Indian male. The canon-revising dispositions of Theorists have, clearly, helped these placings. They certainly explain the rise and rise everywhere of Virginia Woolf – herself, of course, a pioneer of feminist canon-smashing arguments – against the gradual decline on syllabuses of D. H. Lawrence, once the acme of Leavis's Great Tradition and at the summit of Raymond Williams's Marxist readings of the English novel. Just so, the great popularity of Angela Carter in British universities is undoubtedly driven by the spread of feminist Theory (more would-be graduate researchers in Britain applied for funding to work on Angela Carter at the end of the 1990s than on the whole of the eighteenth century put together). And no doubt *Tristram Shandy* comes very high indeed in current neo-lists of Great Fiction because of Theory's predilections for playful and self-referential textuality. And who would have considered putting *Finnegans Wake* on any syllabus were it not for Derrida's and his poststructuralist followers' enthusiasms for it? (Joyce, not in the US top 25 in the 1960s, now ranks at number ten.) Something similar goes for Rabelais, utterly ignored by English Literature students until he sprang into prominent view as the archetype of the cult of the carnivalesque as promoted by Bakhtin's *Rabelais and His World*. And so on.

Naturally enough there's a downside to the canon challenges of Theory in that some one-time favourites fall into the second team or even off the list altogether. And many old books are suffering in universities at the expense of newer ones. The fortunes of many old male authors are now distinctly wobbly. D. H. Lawrence is not the only one whose market share has gone down dramatically. Most of the top 26 NAS authors of 1964–5 have lost ground, including Shakespeare, Milton, Blake, Wordsworth, Eliot, Hardy, with Dryden, Arnold, Ben Jonson, Spenser, Keats, Byron and Coleridge dropping out of the top 25 studied authors altogether. Only Henry James's fortunes have risen at all among the old males. And it is a bit disquieting to see these sharp declines. It's an unhappy consequence of time-constrained undergraduate courses that the more attention paid to *Uncle Tom's Cabin*, the less room there is for Blake. But no one would quarrel, I hope, with the push up into the US top 25 over the last three decades of the female trio Virginia Woolf, Emily Dickinson, and George Eliot, nor greatly regret the consequential decline of, say, the Caroline poet Sir John Suckling (I know he's on the skids because I recently bought a deleted Birmingham University Library edition of his works in a Stratford-upon-Avon bookshop). And it has been important in every way for our sense of literature and culture and aesthetics, of cultural history and tradition, of literary tradition and literary traditions, as well as for our mere literary knowledge and sheer literary pleasure, that we should be able to hear so many once occluded, repressed and lost voices – that the kingdom, the 'knowable community' (in Raymond Williams's phrase), of eighteenth-century poets – to take just one example of these lovely, enlightening expansions – should be more populous than before as a consequence of the diggings and delvings and resurrections of Roger Lonsdale's territorially expansive *Eighteenth-Century Women Poets* anthology.[4]

These expansions of the canons of text and interpretation are good for readers and reading in so many senses. By such new knowledges, occasions for reading delight obviously increase. And much of that delight comes from reader emancipation, the freedom to read what once you could not because it was not there to be read, and the freedom to read in ways formerly blocked off by once current assumptions and practice. J. Hillis Miller is surely right to praise the shaking of the old canons as liberation from a repressive position ('By "repressive" I mean for example forcing a Latino or Thai in Los Angeles, a Puerto Rican in New York, an inner-city black in either city to read only *King Lear, Great Expectations*, and other works from the old canon, and to read them for a "content" and according to theological assumptions that are prescribed beforehand. This is what Joseph Conrad called "The Suppression of Savage Customs", which, as you remember turned into "Exterminate all the brutes".')[5] Edward Said astutely invites us in his *Culture and Imperialism* (1993) to consider how differently an 'Indian or African scholar of English literature reads *Kim*, say, or *Heart of Darkness*', i.e., 'with a critical urgency not felt in quite the same way by an American or British one'. The clear implication is that such Indian or African readings, once ruled out, or formerly just not present among English or American readers, are now ruled in by the presence of postcolonialist Theory – such as Said's own. You, the Brit or American, are now invited to read 'as an Indian', or 'as an African', to read as they did, and do. The new reading will be for you an eye-opener, a new access to interpretative power with those texts. For the Indian or African it will mean empowerment in the sense of hermeneutic status, political justification, and intellectual, emotional satisfaction. 'The emergence of formerly colonial subjects as interpreters of imperialism and its great cultural works has given imperialism a perceptible, not to say obtrusive identity as a subject for study and vigorous revision' (Said, *Culture and Imperialism*). But more than that, such emergences – which apply, *mutatis mutandis*, to women and blacks and gays and all the other subjects of Theory's renovating gaze – undoubtedly provide reading satisfaction to the emergent interpreters, clearly happy to find a fit (often a fit *at last*) between their selfhoods, their emotional proclivities, their ideological and racial dispositions, and so on, and what they are reading – even if the 'fit' is a negative, adversarial one, because this black critic, say, is finding she has to read a white text hostilely.

All this is indeed to acquire a criticism *of one's own*, to echo Virginia Woolf's influential old feminist demand for *A Room of One's Own* – an echo Elaine Showalter sets going in her piece about the links between Afro-American and feminist Theory.[6] Feeling at home in a text and in a theoretical approach – where, as Henry Louis Gates puts it, for his part, for his kind of reader and reading, he can see 'true reflections of our black faces and hear . . . echoes of our black voices'[7] – is clearly a good thing. Something like it is often a key to engaging readers' interests and prompting their desire to 'read on'. Certainly, recognizing the importance, even the necessity, of such a fit as part of the hook, the engagement, the vital contract and contact between text and reader, is of course what puts Irish writing high on the agenda of Irish and Scottish universities, gets 'teenage' novels onto syllabuses for adolescents, and black and chicano and Jewish texts onto lists for ghetto schools; it's why women students want to write theses on women writers, why work on African writers flourishes in Africa, and on Indian writers in India, and so on. Every teacher of literature has tried sneaking up on recalcitrant students with 'fitting' items – druggie poets for dopeheads, prison experiences for prison literature classes, naughty books for naughty boys and girls; all that. Extra-mural teaching is especially educative for literary pedagogues in such matters. But such adaptation policy makes great sense in many teaching situations. And how often do the reminiscences of readers and writers trace their getting hooked on literature to the moment when they found themselves or their circumstances mirrored in a fiction – little Londoner V. S. Pritchett's 'hot horror' as he read *Oliver Twist* (he describes it in his autobiography *A Cab At The Door: Early Years*, 1968); little Edmund Gosse's discovery (it's related in his *Father and Son*, 1907) of pages from a Gothic novel pasted inside a trunk in the family attic recording dangers to females, which made him terribly anxious about his mother who went out alone distributing religious tracts on London omnibuses; or, for that matter, little orphan Jane Eyre's absorption in Bewick's *Birds*, whose illustrations of lonely creatures in icy wastes she feels aptly mirror her own situation at her awful aunt's house.

Reading as very personal, resulting in interpretation as a form of personal testimony or anecdote, can also, though, get out of hand. It evidently worries Edward Said even as he gives it endorsement ('But in what way can we formulate the relationship between culture and imperialism beyond the asseverations of personal testimony?') and strong resistance to the evidential force of mere anecdote rightly animates many critiques of New Historicism – which sets a high evidential value on the anecdotalized encounter. And there is of course the strong line of thought that one of reading's chief missions is to take you out of yourself, to *carry you away* from the self you inhabit, and your own world, and to introduce you to horizons different from your own, to bring you contacts precisely with difference. So that just ministering to people where and how they currently are – in the ghetto so to say of their own immediate selfhood – is to deny reading's scope for enlargement of person and vision and knowledge. And I agree very much with that. The bringing-of-books-to-where-you-are techniques I do see as very much strategies for getting people started on reading who might otherwise remain uninitiated.

But still there is evidently much to be gained in the strong personal encounter, in intimate self-reflections and self-satisfactions in the reading encounter, and not only if they're what entice readers into texts and keep them enticed by reading. And there's no doubt that much of the good of Theory is what it offers in terms of texts to be read and personal authentication and emotional satisfactions to be gained from Theorized ways of reading. There are job-satisfactions for Theorists too (and I'm trying here to keep irony out of my voice). Theory has been a great generator of posts in universities. This is genuinely a part of the new empowerments of Theory. Glad to be gay, glad to be (at last) a paid-up gay critic. Investing in Theory has given many a Theorist a good time. It's no surprise that the 'plaisir' of the text that Roland Barthes theorizes as a reading result should mean orgasmic delight. There's Club Class travel too – the more costly air-tickets hot postcolonialist Theorists insist on claiming even from impoverished Third World hosts (any African or Indian conference organizer is full of gloomy tales of this).

And nothing, I find, is easier to mock than the personalia which have become such a feature of our Theory era. In many deep and serious ways one does not want to hear what happened to postcolonialist Derrida translator Gayatri Chakravorty Spivak when she lectured at the Riyadh University Centre for Girls, or to learn about the arrangement of the chairs at her seminar in Texas, let alone sort out the nature of the talk/lecture/after-dinner speech she carelessly jabbers about in her latest talk/speech/whatever. One is certainly less than prepared to grant the offered parallel between Sudanese clitoridectomy and her own 'ideological victimage' as an Indian female in US universities. These autobiographical buttresses of her readings are less convincing even than Michael Jackson's crocodile tears when attacking child abuse. They refuse to punch their weight. Autobiography makes little critical happen.[8]

'When in doubt, wax autobiographical,' is how Arnold Rampersand puts the matter dyspeptically in the collection of pieces on the rise of critical confessionalism under Theory, *Confessions of the Critics* (1996), edited by Aram Veeser. In David Lodge's joyful Theory novel *Small*

World: An Academic Romance (1984), the egregious Theorist Morris Zapp gives a lecture on 'Textuality as Striptease'. 'Then it was satire', says Gillian Brown in her piece in the Veeser volume, 'Today it is realism'. And do we really want to know about the critic's body-size, hair, car preferences, travel encounters, sex, family, religion, phobias, dreams and diseases? Do they really add value to the criticisms they preface? Aram Veeser thinks they do (his introduction listing such recurrent confessional offerings by critics is entitled 'The Case for Confessional Criticism'). Well, they don't, say I, at least not in such grotesquely massive detail. I like the sense of a real personal reading encounter, and reading as being of the occasion, set in a real place and real time, but it takes far less than I'm usually getting nowadays by way of such admissions, to convince me of that.

I mean, the long confessional run-up to Eve Kosofsky Sedgwick's *Tendencies* (1994) is a characteristic irrelevance, strictly speaking. '*The Golden Bowl*, J. L. Austin, *Dr Susan Love's Breast Book*, and Mme de Sévigné are stacked up, open-faced, on the chair opposite me as I write. I've got three projects braiding and unbraiding in my mind. . . .' ('open-faced' is good: best to open a book before you read it, don't you think?). So What? one wants to cry. Or, Get On With It. We'll be the judge of the results, should they ever come. The self-assertion is obtrusive, the self-naming diverts attention, and usually fails as a kind of authorizing for the criticism that follows. The story of the balletic young brown woman signer for the deaf ignored by all the clever analytical white male speakers but not by the women ones at a Georgetown University conference, with which Elaine Showalter opens her 'Criticism of Our Own' piece I just referred to, makes an entertaining story; and you feel happy for Professor Showalter that the episode helped her feel superior to the academic men who ignored this example of the excluded woman, especially the excluded Third World woman whom feminist and postcolonialist discourse wish to name and identify and bring into the fold of meaning and discourse. But as a case it is more charming than critically illustrative. And, of course, this act of naming and identifying the excluded Other begins in the self-naming of Elaine Showalter. Characteristically of this neck of the Theory woods. The excluded female Other must always be named, insists Gayatri Spivak. 'She must always be acknowledged in our work.' 'Who is the other woman? How am I naming her?' But, also, 'How does she name me?' Not at all, is probably the right answer to that. But Spivak can't ever avoid thinking about herself in these thoughts about the Others. And her namings of the Third World woman Other usually involve the loud naming of herself. The self-promotion going on is intense; the high egotism is clear. The mode is the boast (what Kingsley Amis in his poem about *Beowulf* ('So, bored with dragons . . .') called the *yelp word*). And it's typical of the me-generation effect of Theory. The over-personal story of the personal reading. Autobiography run riot.

Naturally one would expect Eve Kosofsky Sedgwick's now notorious lecture 'Jane Austen and the Masturbating Girl' to cause a fuss. How could it not? It was designed to do so. But now the fuss has become part of the finally published item, down even to Sedgwick making available to us the relevant warring pages from the *New York Times*. This is news, undoubtedly, but news that's not really critically newsworthy; it adds nothing critically, not even Theoretically.[9]

At such over-confessional moments, one's sympathies are intensely with the narrator of Julian Barnes's novel *Flaubert's Parrot* (1985), at the point where, having listed some of the things he likes about France – *pharmacies*, *Beaux-arts* town halls, improbable road-signs like those warning of *betteraves*, beetroots, on the road – he then lays into Roland Barthes's autobiographical book *Barthes par Barthes* (1975).

> I read a list the other day headed 'What I Like'. It went: 'Salad, cinnamon, cheese, pimento, marzipan, the smell of new-cut hay [would you read on?] . . . roses, peonies, lavender, champagne, loosely-held political convictions, Glenn Gould. . . .' The list, which is by Roland Barthes, continues, as lists do. One item you approve, the next stirs irritation. After 'Médoc wine' and 'having change', Barthes approves of '*Bouvard et Pécuchet*'. Good; fine; we'll read on. What's next? 'Walking in sandals on the lanes of south-west France.' It's enough to make you drive all the way to south-west France and strew beetroot on the lanes.[10]

Such strewing or chucking of beetroot is called for much too often in our Theory times. But still, these invitations to us to take a personal interest, these personal boastings and self-identifyings, do indicate the extent to which the various sectional interests of the Theory gumboid bring pleasure – real and legitimate pleasure – to their exponents. And who would not be happy with the way Theory has not just given a voice to former marginal interests and persons in texts, but has given an affirming voice to critics from, or identifying with, those margins? Happiness from and through reading is undoubtedly an absolutely good thing. We're all – I hope – locked into the quest for such bliss. As Julian Barnes is locked into his own making of those lists, or canons, of French goodies, which he packs into his novel – even as he deplores such listings in others.

5

Fragments . . . Ruins

These fragments have I spelt into my ruins
                                 T. S. Eliot, ms. version of *The Waste Land*

But for all the good and goods of Theory, the plain fact is that there are so many downers in and through it. Reading, readers, writers, writing have all suffered dramatically as they've been swept up into the copious embrace, the monstrously loose baggy sack, the gumbo-bowl, the satura lanx, of the linguistic turn and its afterquakes.

Particularly bad is that Theory is carried away by – and seeks to carry reading and readers away with – a tidal wave of hermeneutical suspicion. Theory is an accumulated hermeneutics of suspicion, and one gone rampant, on the rampage. Jonathan Culler's handy little tome *Literary Theory: A Very Short Introduction*, could not be more succinct about this, bullet points and all:

> The main effect of theory is the disputing of 'common sense': common-sense views about meaning, writing, literature, experience. For example, theory questions
>
> - The conception that the meaning of an utterance or text is what the speaker 'had in mind',
> - or the idea that writing is an expression whose truth lies elsewhere, in an experience or state of affairs which it expresses,
> - or the notion that reality is what is 'present' at a given moment.
>   . . .

As a critique of common sense and exploration of alternative conceptions, theory involves a questioning of the most basic premisses or assumptions of literary study, the unsettling of anything that might have been taken for granted: What is meaning? What is an author? What is it to read? What is the 'I' or subject who writes, reads, or acts? How do texts relate to the circumstances in which they are produced?

Suspicion rains down, in other words – and glibly in the great run of cases – upon every area marked out by what I've called the Big Three of traditional poetics. The role of the writer unravels – as Roland Barthes's dismissive wand is waved declaring the Death of the Author. Writing, he declares definitively, writes, not writers. It's not the man who writes the language but the language that writes the man. All that is, is 'written' – 'Il n'y a pas de hors-texte' in that magnetizingly untranslatable but highly quotable slogan from Derrida's *De La Grammatologie* – but this text can't be located with much certainty. Texts are certainly not givens. They are constructed by readers: it's the message, early and late, from Stanley Fish (no message in this text unless I or the 'interpretive community' says so). In any case texts leak, and defy knowable boundaries, overflowing – Derrida again – all boundaries assigned to them. They are, strictly speaking, unreadable for other reasons – their meanings, any linguistic/textual meanings, are always on edge, always 'under erasure'. And if writers die and texts and their meanings fray and disappear then readers are bound to have a very hard time. They have a hard time anyway, because according to the lessons of Freud and Lacan, and Marx and Althusser et al., they have no given nor very fixable identity. The human self is incoherent, broken, split, decentred, polymorphous, a construction site, a stage-set, where selfhood, identity, the *I* that speaks is to be made up – an assembly of personae, parts, roles, variously constrained by desire and ideology and assorted primal scenes and the fall into language, so that the 'I' is a becoming merely, a work in progress, an original compound only of convenient fictions, a set of merely useful stories about my self, that I (and my culture) make and tell myself/

55

ourselves in order to organize ourselves to live by. So reading on such views is an encounter between unstable fictions – the friable readerly self in search of the moving textual target which in any case can only exist courtesy of that rather vain quest. The end of humanism, or Humanism, this bleak vision is called. No wonder reader anxiety is a main result – hyper-anxiety, far worse than the allegorical Anxiety of the Goalie at the Penalty Kick, *Die Angst des Tormanns beim Elfmeter*, so nicely emblematized in Peter Handke's novel (1970) and Wim Wenders's film of it.

The grand Theorists impress by coming up with brilliant illustrations of the practical dilemmas Theorizing's generalizations declare. In his strong reading of that haunting and cryptic part of Kafka's *The Trial* known as 'Before the Law', Derrida turns it into an extraordinary parable of the monumental difficulties of the reader stymied at the very portals of the reading process. The Law in Derrida's interpretation represents literature itself. But this is the literary as the not-known, the indefinable. This Law can't even be named. 'A text of philosophy, science, a text of knowledge or information, would not abandon a name to a state of not-knowing.' But literature does that. And the reader has no chance of ever entering into this place with no certain name. 'We are before this text, that, saying nothing definite and presenting no identifiable content beyond the story itself, except an endless *différance*, till death, nonetheless remains strictly intangible.' Reading is this Kafkan nightmare; it goes nowhere; the reader can't get started; the text is elusive; content endlessly intangible.[1]

Foucault's vivid account of Velasquez's painting *Las Meninas*, with which he opens his deservedly influential *The Order of Things* (1970) – *Les Mots et Les Choses* (1966) – is even more vivid as an exemplum of theory's tripartite reading troubles. Here's the painter representing himself in the very act of painting the Spanish royal family, king, queen, children, dwarves, dogs and all. The act of painting is its own textual subject, is the textual object. Here the work of art retreats from the world, from any outside of text, down, abysmally into its own being. The text is really a metatext. Its selfhood is only a precarious self-referentiality. And so too is the painter, as it were the author.

We see him peering out from behind the canvas he's at work on. He was able to see himself thus in a mirror held up to the artwork. This is a painting not holding up a mirror to life; it exists only in a mirror held up to the work of its own creation as a work of art. So what has enabled the painting act, the business of representation, such as it is, is inward-directed mirrors. The painter can only do and be himself thus, by virtue of looking into mirrors. Self-mirroring is the total condition of the painter's and the painting's world. The would-be main subject, the King and Queen of Spain, are visible only as tiny blurred figures in a tiny mirror at the back of the painted scene. Their high majesties are available to our gaze only as a mirrored reflection thrown back in a painting of a mirrored reflection. Human and aesthetic existence, the human subject and the human object, the painter and the painting (the author and his text), the act of seeing and knowing and representing, could scarcely get much more under erasure, under question, than this. And of course in this labyrinth of complexly ravelled problematics, we, the readers of Velasquez, are in effect standing where the King and Queen 'really' stood. To read this painting we stand before it with the gaze of the painter upon us, precisely in the place of the original subject's erasure. Their erasure, their removal looks at first like our opportunity. The death of the author, the questioning of the text is, as Barthes put it, the birth of the reader. But what price the invitation to read in such a case? If the fate of these potently majestic subjects is to be dissolved into a wilderness of mirrors, of mirages, then we are unlikely to get off lightly. And of course we do not. As we stand there reading the painting, all the anxieties that the painting loads onto its royal subject and upon their artist fall heavily upon us, their majesties' temporary stand-ins, the latest objects of the speculative painted gaze of Velasquez. We readers are what the painting is pointing to, burdened as we look at it with all of its scepticisms and irresolutions – at least as Foucault's bravura analysis brings those readerly anxieties so magnificently home to us.

Pyrrhonism – Theory's multiplied scepticisms of the kind Culler points to – could not be more extreme. Pyrrhonism: named for the very sceptical ancient Greek philosopher, Pyrrho of Elis: a title of honour among some Theorists, who regret any blunting of Theory's sceptical edge wherever that looks like occurring. The New Historicists Stephen Greenblatt and Catherine Gallagher have invoked the 'betrayal' of deconstruction's 'Pyrrhonian energy' as a warning to their kind of critics not to lose the true faith. Any softening of theory's scepticisms is as bad, they suggest, as someone in the seventeenth century trying 'to rewrite [the sceptical] Montaigne in order to make him sound like [orthodox] Thomas Aquinas'.[2] Which is an analogy more potent than they seem to realize. For Montaigne talked about Pyrrhonism, and in connection with a great and frequently invoked example of textuality from the high Christian era – and one Stephen Greenblatt, driven by New Historicism's particular investment in the linguistic turn, is greatly interested in undoing later in the same book – namely the words attributed to Jesus at the Last Supper, when he 'took bread' and 'broke it' and said 'this is my body, broken for you' – words and actions repeated by the priest or minister at every celebration of the Christian eucharist. *Hoc est corpus meum*: this is my body. What did those words signify? What did *hoc/this* point to? To what was Christ referring? The bread? His flesh? What did/does *est/is* mean – especially of the bread in the minister's hand? How is it the 'body' of Christ? In what sense was/is Christ 'really present' in the mass, the eucharist? Here was an absolutely central crux of the Reformation, some of the most contentious words in the whole history of Christian reading (as Greenblatt nicely indicates with the help of Miri Rubin's extremely informative *Corpus Christi: The Eucharist in Late Medieval Culture*, 1991), and ones rightly taken to drive straight to the heart of the ancient language reference problem, the question, central to Theory, of the real presence or otherwise of meaning in words.[3] What do words signify when they appear to point to things ('*This* is . . .')? What is the thisness, the deixis, of language and text? Is there any real presence in words, in text? It's the grand Derridean question. *Tristram Shandy*, the novel perennially close to Theory's linguistic Pyrrhonism, naturally takes the eucharistic contention as central to its probings. And for Michel de Montaigne this is the main illustration of language's difficulties.

58

In a passage in Montaigne's 'Apology for Raymond Sebond', often referred to fondly by Theorists, where he talks of the 'defects and weaknesses' of speech – 'Most of the world's squabbles are occasioned by grammar'; disputations over interpretations of laws lead to law-suits; 'most wars' arise from the confused meanings of conventions and treaties – the clinching example is the much disputed eucharistic formula. 'How many quarrels, momentous quarrels, have arisen in the world because of doubts about the meaning of that single syllable *Hoc*.' Like all of our Theorists, all of them disposed more or less to the extremes of the Pyrrhonism Culler outlines, Greenblatt recruits these traditional disputes over the eucharistic words as underscoring a hermeneutics of necessary suspicion ('A stable ideology of representa-tion is challenged . . .', and the like). No pointing *hoc*, no claim of presented meaning, is safe, it seems, in the shadow of these disputes. But Greenblatt, and the traditions of the Theory he's absorbed, forget that Montaigne – even, or noteworthily, sceptical Montaigne, who was inspired by Pyrrho enough to have the Pyrrhonic inscription 'What do I know?' engraved on the poised balance pictured on his personal medal – goes on immediately to disclaim the absoluteness of the ex-treme scepticism that his observations might appear to have landed him in. 'Pyrrhonist philosophers, I see, cannot express their general concepts in any known kind of speech; they would need a new lan-guage: ours is made up of affirmative propositions totally inimical to them – so much so that when they say "I doubt", you can jump down their throats and make them admit that they at least know one thing for certain, namely that they doubt'.[4]

Theorists pick and choose conveniently and arbitrarily from their copies of Montaigne's essays. (I shall argue at some length, later, that Theorists are, as a class, bad readers.) Montaigne's scepticism about scepticism is inconvenient for Theory. For it is indeed hard to deny language its claims on real presence, to disclaim the force of language's deictic desires, of the thisness, the individuating *haecceitas* (as Duns Scotus and Gerard Manley Hopkins would put it) of things and per-sons repeatedly pointed to by the *hoc est* of texts, even though the difficulties and contentiousness of such claims have always to be registered as a matter of critical course. But our neo-Pyrrhonists are not to be deterred by their exemplar's wise and proper, indeed scathing, cautions. So much so, that an extraordinary barrage of Pyrrhonist rhetoric has in recent Theory times quite battered the notion of literary communication almost to death.

Under Theory, the text is demonized by a clamantly Pyrrhonistic rhetoric of lapse, failure, lack, disablement, deficiency. This rhetoric of deploring is all over the pages of Theorists. The text is in ruins, a ruin, a bomb-site. How animated Theorists have been by Walter Benjamin's laconic words about allegory (which is taken as meaning the poetic, the textual) as being in the realm of thought what ruins are in the world of things.[5] The text according to Theory is fragmented, bitty, broken. It can't speak out; it stutters; it hesitates; it can't see; it's blind; it's occluded. It's disfigured, defaced, an affair of de-facing, of de-personifying (whereas *prosopopoiea* – face-making, the making of selves, personification – is thought of traditionally as the work of writing): an influential deconstructive line, this, of Paul de Man's.[6] The text does not know itself; it's unconscious of what it's up to; it's repressed. It can't walk straight; it staggers; it's lame; it's maimed; it errs. The text misleads: it's labyrinthine; amazing; aporetic. The job your common-sense (Culler) has you thinking writing is there for – communication, description of the real and the human, insight, knowledge, companionship, consolation, moral effect, emotional affect – all of which writing blatantly pretends to be about, is simply not being done. Theory looks for textual model to the worst-case stories, the most notorious examples and allegories of the darkening of counsel and the confusions and occlusions of meaning: the dark navel of the Freudian dream text; the tower of Babel, where human speech was 'confused'; Moses breaking the tablets of the Law; Moses's stuttering prophecies; wrestling, limping Jacob; the story of the enemies of Israel who have to die because they're unable to utter the word *shibboleth*; Theseus in the maze of King Minos; Oedipus's delusions; Hamlet's doubtings; the narrative failures in general of Conrad's Marlow and *Heart of Darkness*'s extended rhetorics of the unspeakable in particular; *Finnegans Wake*, the largest ever text of hesitation (or HeCitEncy).

Walter Benjamin and Harold Bloom and Paul de Man and Derrida all variously take as basic the kabbalistic, mystical rabbinical idea of the text as beginning in an original brokenness, *The Breaking of the Vessels*.

And worse still, these deficiencies are seen as corrupted ones, as criminal acts. It's no accident that those going literary models of the the failure of signification tend to be, variously, stories of wronging, wrong, crime, transgression. The text is a criminal occasion; it criminalizes; it abets and affirms the reader's own criminality. Of necessity Theory accuses the text of crime, arraigns it before the dock of righteous criticism, affirms its guilt. The text arises as a result of oppression; it's in the pay of malign institutions, wicked state apparatuses, false consciousness; it's the agent of oppressions, repressions, subjugations. It needs careful policing and, naturally, psychoanalytic treatment. It's sick, unwell, a bunch of infections. It's slippery; a place of meaning slippage; a place where the reader can easily slip up. You've got to watch it or it will get you, mug you, take you in in some very nasty way, unawares, if you wander naively down its dark textual alleys. It can lead you astray morally, politically, linguistically. So if you don't read the text against its warped grain you'll end up confirmed in its ideological duplicities and mess. The magic that texts want to work on you is highly suspect. Their music is the dangerous Song of the Sirens. These delusive spells must be broken. 'The story, however pleasurable or absorbing, is shoring up ideological propositions or confirming the legitimacy of institutional propositions or confirming the legitimacy of institutional arrangements.'[7]

Reading on Theory's model, or models, is then a matter of good readerly intentions, good faith, encountering a kind of textual bad faith, the malfeasance of the literary. Julian Wolfreys's cannily garnered *Readings: Acts of Close Reading in Literary Theory* (2000), a relishable A–Z of Theory-promoters (everyone from Althusser down to Žižek), in which Wolfreys sharply reads the texts of Theorizing readers on the subject of reading, makes this widespread vision of reading as a Sisyphean uphill struggle utterly clear. (The clarity is a paradox indeed about the most exhilaratingly Pyrrhonic roller-coaster of a Theory volume around.) The book is dedicated to J. Hillis Miller, who is doubtless expected to approve of the roster of negativity it registers. Reading is a crime, a guilty work (Althusser). It's a fine and private place, like an adulterous bed or the grave in Marvell's poem *To His Coy Mistress*, where lies and illicit satisfactions abound (Francis Barker). It's where misinterpreting reader meets the poem misinterpreting another poem (Harold Bloom). It's a matter of remains, torn-up pages, what's left of ruination – perhaps (Hélène Cixous). It's eating forbidden fruit (Cixous, again; who elsewhere, in her book *Three Steps on the Ladder of Writing*, 1993, claims death as the writer–reader's constant point of origin). It's *clôtural* – in-fin-ite, 'without end, apocalypse, *eschaton*' (Simon Critchley). It's a failed attempt at textual mastery, like a dredging machine, scraping the seashore-bed, picking up a few stones, some algae, but mainly water which falls out of the dredger's mouth as soon as it's gathered up (Jacques Derrida). It scatters your selfhood across others' pages, inducing *stultitia*, stupidity (Michel Foucault). It's an encounter with unreadable fragments, interruptions, the not-there, with bits that say far less than they should (Hans-Jost Frey). It's a swindle, a confidence trick, a credit-card with no apparent limit, promising everything but always not yet (Peggy Kamuf). It 'destroys the traditional categories of the book as a closed totality containing a definite meaning' (Sarah Kofman). Like infectious laughter, its infectiousness is difficult 'to bring under control' (D. Farrell). It's a matter of encountering the signifier's slips and so a matter of difficulty, going awry, even of 'not reading at all' (Jacques Lacan). It is 'never finished' (Jean-François Lyotard). It's always 'between', as in an interlinear text (Rainer Nägele: copying Walter Benjamin). It's where meaning 'strains against the burden of meaning and throws it off balance' – a forever merely beginning process, 'an *incipit* that is always begun again' (Jean-Luc Nancy: his theme tune, obviously, the favourite postmodernist one 'I Can't Get Started'). It's avoidance of reading (Thomas Pepper). 'Reading . . . must not claim to reveal hidden meaning' (Bill Readings). It promises 'future illumination. But it is a future that will never have completed its task in the present' (Avital Ronell). It 'always remains to be read' (Nicholas Royle, *After Derrida*). It's disfiguring, misappropriative, anachronistic (Slavoj Žižek).

The book has no entry under W – Wolfreys keeps his own alpha-
betical portion out of his alphabet, like Roland Barthes omitting any
actual photo of his mother in the death-of-his-mother haunted book
Camera Lucida. But, like Barthes's mother, Wolfreys is everywhere,
closely reading these discounters of the old alleged results of close
reading, to the end of perpetually endorsing this massed choir of
Pyrrhonists. 'We keep reading close, even though it gets away from
us' (Wolfreys on Ronell). Reading on this plan is always metaleptic,
an endless elusive process of substitution, and not of thisness, but
only of mere metaphors, figures of thisness (Wolfreys on Ronell,
again). Reading considered thus hears the *Hoc est meum corpus*, but
the body, the host, the would-be nourishing edibilium, is only words
and more words for real things, but never the things themselves. All,
as it were, rhetorical ashes in the mouth. Reading always takes you
close to meaning; you are always in meaning's neighbourhood
(Wolfreys again). But you're never let all that close. Like being invited to touch the (after all) intangible in Derrida's reading of 'Before
the Law'.

Cannily (he's all Theoretical canniness, this master of the Theory of
textual bittiness), Wolfreys's texts are all without exception little extracts, torn-off bits, his gathering a tessellation, a merely tessellated
Theoretical pathway: vivid demonstration that even the closest attempt at Theorized close reading will be a close encounter of the
fragmented kind, all starting and abrupt stopping, a stuttering indeed.
Wonderfully clear though Wolfreys's own readings can be, they're
always clear only about the possibility of nothing but stuttering. And
they themselves often go in for a kind of stylistic stuttering of the sort
their admired target texts frequently practise. Which is scarcely sur-
prising. It's practising what you preach.

And Theorists do like trying to practise what they preach, at least
stylistically. So it's no surprise to find lots of those preaching up only
the opacity–capacity of texts, getting besotted by it as a critical style.
No stratagem is easier than to poke fun at Theory's yen for clottedness
and opacity, its love of startling neologizing and so on, the sheer jan-
gling dissonance of some of its language. Such accusations are the first

resort of conservatives of all kinds, as they sniff, for example, through the titles of the annual convention of the Modern Languages Association of North America on the lookout for rebarbative novelties and the lingo-twisting conjunctions which are supposed to mark the wit of Theory. And to be sure the MLA programme does make easy pickings for mockery as it holds a mirror up to Theory's investment in the freeplay of the neologism, its joyful mating of strange Theory bedfellows, its zesty yoking of not-quite heterogeneous Theory elements together by violence through the energies of Theory's inspirations. 'Girling Popular Culture.' 'Crossover Tongues: Bilingual Sexuality.' 'Logomarginality among Shakespeare's Speakers and Listeners.' 'Vicarious Witness in *Beloved*: "Plurisignant" Tragedy and the Footprints' Fit.' 'The Anal Eye of Ecstacy.' 'Contemporary American Literature in the Age of the "Post-" as/and "Multi-".' 'The Medusa Complex: Big Hair, Bad Hair, and Russian Women Authors of the Fin de Siècle.' I liked all of these (from the MLA's 2000 programme), all showing people strutting their stuff in the high chutzpah spirit of Monty Python's Hell's Grannies asking for trouble from the NAS. But none of these (and scores and scores of others like them) are worried enough about questions of what we might call critical measure and rhetorical tact.

I myself see no clear reason why words in *-ize* or *-icity* should act as the reddest rag to bullish conservatives, such as Roger Shattuck in his *Candor and Perversion: Literature, Education and the Arts* (1999: 'Let us desist from referring to '*the canon*', or canons or – God save us – canonicity'). (I want to use the very useful *canonicity* all the time.) And Theorists are right to turn the tables on anyone who wants to suggest mere barbarity of tongue, by invoking the great load of Graeco-Romano-British racism the charge bears. *Barbaros, barbarus, barbarian*: the stuttering foreigner whose speech is a glossalalic stammering, *ba-ba-ba-ba*, in the ears of a Greek, then of a Roman, then of an Englishman, and so the utterance of people self-defined as outlandish, foreign, strange, not one of us. You now call me *barbaric* at your moral and political peril. But what if I deliberately cultivate dissonance, Babelism, glossalalia, the *Unheimlich*, uncanniness of tongue, as the essence of text and reading – and even claim *mumbo-jumbo* as the character of my would-be revolutionary critical discourse? Which is what Henry Louis Gates does, admittedly with the understandable aim of subverting the white-man-imperialist's hostile labellings – just as *nigger* and *queer* have been taken back from their detracting users and recycled as honorific terms.

But this is a dangerous stylistic game to play – a kind of leading with the chin, as boxers would say. For the reclaimed *mumbo-jumbo*, snatched adroitly back from its 'ethnocentric Western' denigrators, and celebrated by Gates as the essence of the Afro-Americanized Shandeyesque and Joycean stylistic excitements in Ishmael Reed's novel *Mumbo Jumbo* (1972) – 'the dazzling parodying punning mischievous pre-Joycean style-play of your Cakewalking your Calinda your Minstrelsy give-and-take of the ultra-absurd' – still hovers dauntingly on the edge of its standard dismissive English meaning: gibberish.

I don't want to say that Theorists write gibberish. But they can get pretty close. Reading Lacan, for example, one can't help being re-minded sometimes that in his early career he was a Surrealist – an endorser of, well, poetic gibberish in the name of the vocalized un-conscious. And Theoretic ephebes do rather go in for quasi-gibberish in tribute to the Grand Masters. This is job-cred in some academic circles, a set of passwords to the club. This is what so many of the youthie MLA titles are shouting out loud: Let me in, I can talk like you. How, for example, nouns all broken up with dashes and brackets proliferated barbarically in the 1970s and 1980s in homage to Lacan's and Derrida's liking for them. All an unnecessary obfuscatory stutter. Here, for example, is Nicholas Royle, wonderfully intelligent Derrida devotee, in his book *After Derrida* (1995), stammering away in loving homage and parody of Derrida's (self-confessed) 'stammering' on the subject of Samuel Beckett's (stammering) writing:

Complete madness. The madness of the day. A light unlike any other. I posthume as I breathe. Folly. Sheer kink. Nothing more or less than a folly to suggest that it could be appropriate to characterise Derrida's work in terms of a maintenance of

65

identity or authority, of a legitimation of the violence of self-authentication, of a persistence of the violence of self-authorisation, of a persistence in valorising the writing 'I'. What is the word? Folly. In ruins. Beckett and Derrida, these two ghosts – each of them like every ghost, double and more than double – are up to the same thing, in their different ways. If Beckett's work shows how – in Bersani's words – 'the strategies for continuing talk survive the absence of psychological subjects', Derrida's work is likewise concerned with working through the deconstitution of psychological subjects, but *from the perspective of their presence*, from the experience of self-presence and, indeed, of *narcissism*. Derrida says as much, for example in that ghostly polyphonic text, 'Right of Inspection', which calls for 'a new understanding of narcissism, a new "patience", a new passion for narcissism'.[8]

The repertoire of key Theory touchstones here – ruin, self, presence, absence, deconstitution, polyphony, as well as the stepping into Theory's favoured autobiographical critical mode ('I posthume . . .') – are all fascinating. This is not, of course it's not, 'complete madness'. But it is not plain, and its lack of plainness is narcissistic, and deliberate, and paying careful *hommage* to the Theory tradition in its wilful gibbering. No one demands, I hope, absolute plainness of style as a necessary requirement of critical writing, but deliberate crypticity, stuttering by choice, should not be surprised if it attracts vexation over its obfuscations.

Milton's irritation with Bible commentators who loaded what was for him the plain sense of scripture with complex allegorical meanings comes to mind again in the presence of many a Theory-driven commentator, including the greatest ones:

Through what madness is it, then, that even members of the reformed church persist in explaining and illustrating and interpreting the most holy truths of religion, as if they were conveyed obscurely in the Holy Scriptures? Why do they shroud them in the thick darkness of metaphysics? Why do they employ all their useless technicalities and meaningless distinctions and barbarous jargon in their attempt to make the scriptures plainer and easier to understand . . . as if the sense of the divine truth, itself absolutely plain, needed to be brought out more clearly or more fully, or otherwise explained, by means of terms imported from the most abstruse of human sciences. . .[9]

I do not wish to imply that Theory and its terms are useless and meaningless, far from it. And, as everyone knows, one person's jargon is another person's technical terminology. And, of course, imports and neologisms often make themselves utterly at home in their target language, and can soon lose their first air of rebarbative foreignness. And one sign of the spread of Theory is how the key terms, even ones in, or *calques* on, languages other than English come to seem pretty natural ones (see the NAS list). So that no one much remembers, or feels they need to remember that, say, *signifier* arrived as an American translation (Wade Baskin's) of Saussure's *signifiant*; and no one notices that Saussure's *binaries* started as a metaphor from the Italian word for railway lines, *binari*, picked up from his regularly standing on Swiss railway stations; and no one is very certain who actually started the great hare of *otherness* which we now hear so very much about; and no student wishes to be told any more that *aporia* is a Greek term of rhetoric. For all these items are acclimatized, naturalized among us; they've lost their foreignness. Did I credit Paul Ricoeur when I used the phrase 'hermeneutics of suspicion'? No, I forgot, and didn't need to; the phrase and the idea are simply at home now; they're in the regular critical parlance, mere tools of the everyday critical trade, barbarous no longer. ('Play some traditional', people used to shout in the later 1950s from the balcony seats at Birmingham Town Hall or wherever as Chris Barber's Traditional Jazz Band first brought in the 'dirty bopper' Bruce Turner and his 'modernist' tenor sax. Very shortly Bruce Turner was sounding rather traditional himself.) But still some accusations of the darkenings of an abstruse metaphysics, the obtuseness of imported sentences, and some of that

67

indignation about barbarity of Theory-derived tongue, stick because they are pertinent.

Even the Bible, said the rabbis, must speak 'in the language of men', as Geoffrey Hartman reminds us in one of the more rhapsodic parts of his book *The Fate of Reading*.[10] Theory's conceptual gumbo too readily plays onto linguistic mumbo-jumbo – and All That Jazz.

6

All What Jazz? Or, The Incredibly Disappearing Text

On me your voice falls as they say love should,
Like an enormous yes. My Crescent City
Is where your speech alone is understood.
        Philip Larkin, 'For Sidney Bechet', *The Whitsun Weddings*

You can see why jazz – improvisatory, free, even on occasion free-play – excites Theory's model-seekers of all sorts, as well as the Afro-American writers and critics whose very own music it is. 'Telmah', the lovely riffing piece on *Hamlet* by Terence Hawkes, a jazz drum-mer as well as founding contributor to the Theory-evangelizing and pioneering Methuen New Accents series of critical texts, nicely offers jazz improvisation as a model for Shakespearian actors' improvisings, and so also for the improvisable meanings of texts such as *Hamlet*, and for the improvisatory nature of reading (a set of suggestions spoiled as well as cheekily enhanced by Hawkes's play with the name Fortinbras – *fort/bras* – strong/arm – [Louis] Armstrong).[1] But improvising, busk-ing, making it up as you go along, playing as you please, taking off with freedom from the written score, the 'notes', as jazz-players say, though it is mightily attractive to Theorists as critical example, is not exactly a recipe for doing well, as well as one should, or might, by texts. And so it has proved. Theory is, all too often, bad for texts, not only because its models of their being, their ontology, their essence, their nature, are driven by a huge negativity and despair, but because

69

of how it promotes a view of text and so of readings of texts which plays fast and loose with the idea and then also the praxis of a demanding textual thereness. Theory is variously careless of the texts it will keep asserting it cares about and which are its great object, however despairingly or with whatever degree of absurdism that caring comes qualified. Bluntly, Theory practically denigrates the literary object by now pretending it's not really there, now by devotedly circumventing or side-stepping it, now by smothering it to death with excesses of attention.

In every way, the result is The Incredibly Disappearing Text.

Theory wipes the textual slate clean. Theory banishes texts. Canon warfares are about expunging, sponging away undesirables, as defined by Theory, getting rid of DWEMs, old Big Books, classics, the kin and cousinhood of the DWEM. Theory gets its kathartic kicks from canon purging. It's a kind of updating of Third Reich book-burning. 'To the stake!' is the cry. (One keen US student of mine told me he'd been informed by his teachers that Augustine was a Dead White European Male. Well he is dead, and he was male. But he wasn't European. Hippo, his birthplace, is in North Africa. He probably looked like a cousin of Colonel Gaddafi. Another student, a high-flying black woman, told me Graham Swift's novel *Last Orders* (1996) was the first book by a white male that she'd been made to read in an academic context.) Here's *Another One to Cross Off Your List*, Theory keeps saying, as F. C. Crews has his F. R. Leavis character Simon Lacerous saying in the lovely satire on mid-twentieth century critical practices, *The Pooh Perplex: A Student Casebook* (1964). Theory's Simon Lacerouses are keen *poubellistes*, garbage-disposal persons. But even when texts survive Theory's purges, they do so crucially orphaned.

In Theory's view, the text is not all there. It's not all there in every sense, including the popular one meaning mentally deficient. It's 'lacking' as we say; even just not there at all. The literary object so confidently named by Matthew Arnold, for whom the critical act is the (repeatedly put) effort to see the object 'as in itself it really is'; the tangible, handlable, knowable, object of commonsensical readerly attention, of ordinary readerly expectation and experience (I sit down with *Moby Dick*; I go to the theatre to see *The Duchess of Malfi*; I tell my students they will read *Great Expectations* next week; this TV programme is an adaptation of Kingsley Amis's novel *Take A Girl Like You*; I write about Derrida's *Memoirs of the Blind*), is, under Theory's complex gaze, seen as eviscerated, holed, fragmented, a set of absences, of not-therenesses. It's full of holes, though it might profess wholeness. It's an affair of cracks, gaps, interruptions, gawpings, like a piece of Emmental cheese or a strip of meccano. 'Reading is always this, the experience of fragmentation': thus Wolfreys commenting in his *Readings* on Hans-Jost Frey's declarations in his *Interruptions* (1996) about what this fragmentariness means. 'Something is not there, and this lack must be read as well.' But more than just this dwelling on lacks in texts – and in such discussions it's not only Theory's favourite modernist texts, Eliot's *The Waste Land*, and Kafka's *The Trial*, and Saussure's *Cours*, which have holes in them – this Theory-line goes on to suggest that lack, gap, *béance* (those gaping mouths of Lacan's intense devotion) are all there is. There's no textual *there* there, except in a kind of paradox which would make emptiness, non-being, into a kind of presence – *opaque emptiness* as Wolfreys glosses it, able to be talked about by the critic, but only as 'talk *about what is not there*'.

You get to this kind of vision only by courtesy of many Theory assumptions, or ways and byways – via the post-Saussurean notion of perpetual difference, the alleged perpetual elusiveness of the signifying chain, the idea of the textual *mise en abyme* instead of the *mise-en-scène*, the ratting on the idea of presence, the interest in textual marginality and borders and decentrings, the push away from fullness, or *pleroma*, to its edgy, marginal, emptied, emptying opposite, and all of this aided by other potent denials and curtailings (authors, canonicity, transcendence, and so on). Too, there's assistance from a kind of chronological bad faith, the pretence that certain great fragmentary texts of modernism, culminating in *Finnegans Wake* (or in certain areas of *Finnegans Wake*, like pages 260–308, where text and marginal notes and footnotes all accumulate to assault the idea of textual uniqueness, centredness, certainty and givenness), are the only proper kinds of text, the goal that all textual experiment is leading to, the great *telos*

71

of all writing. And jogging about in the anglophone background of this francophone alleging is the would-be documentary evidence supplied by Stanley Fish's notorious *Is There a Text in this Class*?

Fish's pretty scenario in 'How to Recognize a Poem When You See One' – the more or less random list of linguists' names on the blackboard left over from his earlier linguistics class (Jacobs-Rosenbaum, Levin, Thorne, et al.); the drawing of a line around the list; the instruction to his seventeenth-century poetry class to read the framed words as a seventeenth-century religious poem; their readiness and skill in doing so – is taken as proving that poems have no intrinsic essence or features. Readers find poeticity when they're told it's present, however unlikely these 'poetic' materials might otherwise seem. There's no necessary poetic there. The poem and poeticity arrive by readers bringing these with them and importing them into the writing. The poem is a blank sheet, or one full of neutral items turned into poeticity because the 'interpretive community' says so. 'Interpretation is not the art of construing but the art of constructing. Interpreters do not decode poems; they make them.' But there was indeed a very real 'there' there, a textual object, one written down by Stanley Fish, its most real author, and in effect published by him, as a poem. This is a poem, and in a seventeenth-century metaphysical genre, he said, putting a mark, a line, around his written-down words, and labelling the contents with a particular generic name. And that is exactly how poems arrive, contained in a frame of some sort – on a page, in a book, at a reading – labelled poems or poetry. (It was in 'a blue poetry book', when he read it, Ginger the airman insists to his new wife in Evelyn Waugh's novel *Vile Bodies* (1930), when she quotes a bit of Shakespeare, so it must be poetry. Fish's word and his chalked framing defined his poem as poem as precisely as any blue poetry book.) And the words had meaning not just after the students got to work on them, but before they got written down, and after they got inscribed, well before the students came into the room. The students read the words intelligently, responded to the intelligences present in the words, to their intelligibility, responded to the conjunction of the words, their form, as well as to the suggested genre of this little text. They riffed, and improvised; for reading is – remember – jazzing along. But they were not busking on nothing.

For 'nothing', in the good words of King Lear to Cordelia, 'will come of nothing'. There is no improvising on 'fuck-all', to borrow the words of Kingsley Amis's poem attacking modernist jazz, 'Farewell Blues' ('Keyless, barless, poor man's Boulez, improvising on fuck-all'). Improvisation always requires a given melody/theme/chord-sequence as base (really 'free jazz' isn't so much improvisation as composition). The only thing proved by the Fish vignette is that the intentions of authors can't ever limit interpretation: Fish could not predict how his students would go on with his little poem, and nor can any other authors.[2]

Raymond Tallis, the medic and literary theorist Theorists love to hate, quotes a medical aphorism: 'The plural of anecdote is not fact'.[3] Fish has only got one anecdote to claim as fact, but it's become a foundational one for his career-long ad libbing on it. Wordsworth's meanings are entirely the 'product' of a 'significant number of workers in the profession'. 'Linguistic and semantic density is not something poems announce, but somethings that readers actualize.'[4] And so on. Only by wilful myopia and the supply of dodgy straw-man definitions of what textual 'objectivity' means can Fish carry the day to his satisfaction (he's very good, i.e. bad, with straw men).

> The objectivity of the text is an illusion and, moreover, a dangerous illusion, because it is so physically convincing. A line of print or a page is so obviously *there* – it can be handled, photographed, or put away – that it seems to be the sole repository of whatever value and meaning we associate with it . . . This is of course the unspoken assumption behind the word 'content'. The line or page or book *contains* – everything.[5]

And he goes on to urge us not to get confused by the spatial appearance of the poem or book into forgetting that reading is a kinetic affair. But who ever forgot that? And who ever really thought the poem was a container of items for a clean and simple extraction job?

Or that poems came out in the same way, in the same order, to the same effect and affect, for all readers, everywhere, ever? No one thought that who had any sense of the perpetually different readings the literary classics – or even the merest rhyme or ditty – have received, and receive. But to deny all intrinsic, pre-readerly meanings to the poetic container's contents is to defy all linguistic logic, as well as the evidence of reading history. You cannot make bricks without straw. There's always got to be something there to start with, or on. And when, as so often, that textual something is fragmented, scattered, full of gaps and verbal betweennesses and possible variants – as *The Waste Land*, or the (now) two version of *King Lear*, or the two texts of *Isaiah*, or the text of Genesis after German Higher Criticism got to work on its huge roster of alphabetically named authors (Harold Bloom's J-Author and all the rest), or *Hamlet* (well, is Hamlet's flesh too too *solid*, or *sullied*, or s*allied*?), or any other poor poetic things you come across in critical edition after critical edition quite studded with textual variation and (often massive) difference – it is nonetheless simply wrong, stupid even, to deny a certain object-status, the authority of a certain, and necessary, givenness. Textual instability, even extreme instability, is not a nothing. Far from it. The problem of textual variants isn't that they generate absence of meaning, but rather that they produce an excess of it. (See how such richnesses mount up, for instance, just one instance, in Jack Stillinger's *Coleridge and Textual Instability: The Multiple Versions of the Major Poems* (1994).)

Reading is just not reading at all if it thinks it can get by all on its own without some textual givenness to work on. Theory which dictates otherwise is misleading. And practice, in effect, inevitably undercuts that Theoretical urging – even if it's only that the textual illustrations which are offered as proof of absence actually prove themselves to be evidences of presence. Stanley Fish's argument proceeds only by courtesy of his little poem's real presence. Wolfreys's lexicon of absence-arguments is present to us only in the passages, the little texts, he chooses for his acts of neo-practical criticism. Derrida's thoughts about the real absence of the literary object are spun out of reflection on a very present fragment of Kafka. Fictions which are

74

taken as recipes for/allegories of absence, like Kafka's 'Before the Law' (*Tristram Shandy* is a much-referred-to case), need their manifest textual presences in order to begin to manifest anything like a prospect of textual elimination and blanking out. *Shandy*'s notorious black page and blank page, great signifiers of occlusion and absence, are both of them manifestly present. If this be absence, it's of a curiously *opaque* kind (to borrow Wolfreys's word).

Which doesn't stop suspicions about textual thereness taking some dramatic forms. As some Theorists enthusiastically deny texts a positive being, so the enthusiasms of others act out the denial by directing critical energy and attention around and beyond the place where it might be thought (common-sense again) to reside. New Historicism is especially adept at this by-pass method. In what has become a highly refined set of practices, Theory's textual refocusings become a sort of wilful overlooking. Texts are acknowledged as sites of meaning, only to be practically circumnavigated. They become places for the immediate displacement of attention elsewhere, for the instant relocating of the reading effort. So in the name of freshened-up reading, especially of high canonical literary texts, readerly attention is actually distracted, made to swerve away from where it purports to be directed, and onto parallel, allegedly analogous, contemporary and not-so contemporary texts, usually of a non-literary, non-fictional, documentary kind. These other texts are, in general, admittedly full of historical, social and anthropological interest – especially interest coming up from below, as it were, from where the disempowered, the marginalized, the rebels and transgressors are, the people with the 'lost voices', shut out of or silenced in the grander narratives prompted by orthodoxy, official authority, churches, kings, emperors and other elevated speakers. This attending to such voices – prompted of course by Foucault and the *annales* school of French history, as well as by the great Marxized English social, and local, history movement led by E. P. Thompson – is important to any sense of the cultural past. It's always most instructive, and necessary I'd say, to have literary texts rescued from a grand isolation and inserted into the times and places and ideologies in which they were seeded and grew. There is no literary text without a highly intricate set of related contexts. And there is positive gain, in readerly knowledge and understanding, when you read, say, Shakespeare's *Henry IV* against writings about the Elizabethan colonists in Virginia; or *Twelfth Night* against contemporary discussion of homosexual marriage, trans-sexuality and hermaphroditism; or *King Lear* against a contemporary denunciation of Roman Catholic exorcism practices. These are all rightly influential revelatory cases from Stephen Greenblatt, guru and founder of New Historicism (he's the coiner of the term). It is not, as Greenblatt keeps insisting, that these contextualizings merely involve what used to be labelled 'influences' or 'sources' – though that possibility often hovers in the air of these discussions. 'The relation I wish to establish between medical and theatrical practice is not one of cause and effect or source and literary realization. We are dealing rather with a shared code, a set of interlocking tropes and similitudes that function not only as the objects but as the conditions of representation.' Thus Greenblatt hovering, contextualizing Theory in hand, around *Twelfth Night*.

Where all this is coming from is clear enough. It's the old Marxist's magpie clutch, Marxianly stressing the conditions of literary production, but combining it now with neo-formalist talk of social encodings which goes back to the relieved-Marxist poststructuralisms of Roland Barthes's *S/Z* (1970 in French, 1974 in English), hepped up by a kind of Foucauldian allegiance to discourse (social and textual and intertextual) as all intratextual and so all rhetorical ('tropes and similitudes'). And these Theoretical scrimpings and scrapings are neither individually nor even collectively derisive. The clear effect, though, is the reduction in status and power of *Twelfth Night* itself, the diversion of attention away from the literary piece onto other texts of its time. The play formerly known as a masterwork of English literature, worthy of close attention 'in itself', regarded as a big text compared to which other texts around it, the textual population of its context(s), were once thought considerable only as supplementary, as adjuncts usefully informative but only as tribute bringers and homage bearers, is utterly subsumed into that context. Its particular 'textual traces' (Greenblatt is fond of the phrase) have been absorbed into the wider textual tracings of the Renaissance.[6]

This might satisfy some admirable democratic sensibilities on the critic's part, and assuage her/his understandable desire to resist imperiousness and imperialism wherever they occur, even when they surround grand cultural items. And bringing down the mighty from their pedestals does have its place in politics, even if it has a less obvious place in cultural politics. And this democratic resistance to what we might call the *timocracy* of aesthetic work does fly in the face of the way canons, lists of preferred works, get formed because readers recognize (as they always have done) that some writings are more excellent than others (however that excellence is variously measured).[7] But whatever one thinks of the allegation that writings like *Twelfth Night* have only had attention paid to them by readers because they stand out from the crowd of their rivals by virtue of their recognized timocratic worths, it remains the case that the clear result of Greenblatt's analysis and his kind of analysis is the devaluing of *Twelfth Night* as an object of readerly attention. A reading and a reader looking elsewhere, and directed both in practice and in principle to look elsewhere, are obviously not, for the moment at least, for this critical moment, looking at *Twelfth Night*. These are diversion tactics. They're not even a kind of bracketing fire – which would aim for the putative target text, but gradually, getting a siting on it, approaching closer and closer by gradually first knocking out the texts on either side of it. On the New Historical method, there is, in effect, only a depleted sense of a main target, even though one keeps being cited; in this reading scenario the whole contemporary scene is the target – all spread out now, all a circumference without a centre, all a supplement. This is in effect a late twist on *il n'y a pas de hors-texte*: here everything is *hors-texte*; here there's no text which isn't merely context.

Of course in these discussions there is constant talk of bridges and leaps and connecting tissue uniting the now overwhelmingly interesting context with the once specially interesting text. And Greenblatt even takes on the ready accusation that as bracketing fire, or creeping barrages go (creeping barrage being that shelling which gradually works up to a target, usually ahead of attacking infantry), these approach shots should be thought of as very naughty ones, indeed, even, in

77

military terms, rather dubious ones, given the way they can start astonishingly far from the alleged target. 'It may be objected' – thus
Greenblatt, stating the obvious – 'that there is something slightly ab-
surd in likening such moments' [Prince Hal's glossings of tavern slang
in *1 Henry IV*] to the glossings of Algonquin Indian speech in Thomas Harriot's *Brief and True Report of the New Found Land of Virginia*
(1588). But Shakespeare's 'theatre is itself a *social event* in reciprocal
contact with other social events'. Thus the excuse for the large leap
from a book about colonizing Virginia to a play about the taverns of
London. But the rationale is lame. The fact of Shakespeare's play in-
habiting the social world in which it is an event doesn't mean it in-
habits any and every bit of that world, and has family ties with any and
every other textual event of its time. Of course, Harriot's book is not
just any old book of the time; but it's almost any old book. Choosing
it was not absolutely arbitrary, but almost so. Which makes a non-
sense even of context as defined by Greenblatt – textual frame; textual
grounding; conditions of literary production; really shared tropes and
similitudes; all those things. This is a wild kind of contextualizing,
casual and uninstructed about interpretative relevance, a dim-witted
epistemology, altogether too happy at its potential for boundlessness.
'I want to begin this essay far from the Renaissance': thus Greenblatt
opening an approach to King Lear's disinheriting of Cordelia with a
reading of the taming of a recalcitrant child in the *American Baptist
Magazine* of 1831 by the Revd Francis Wayland, Baptist minister and
early President of Brown University. Historical and hermeneutic gaps
could scarcely yawn wider. The context's borders have now disappeared right over the horizon of possible relevance and instruction.
This really is any old example of parent authoritarianism and child
disciplining. Of truly slight connection with *King Lear*, raising it slights
the very idea of a text's meaningful context and of any useful
historicizing of reading; but even more it slights the sense of the importance, the relevance of *King Lear*, the play, or plays.

But then, slighting the canonical text, throwing critical light away
from it, is the intention of this highly Theorized method. 'You'll
never get to heaven on roller-skates', the ribald used to sing, because

'You'll roll right past those pearly gates'. The Greenblatt technique is a rolling right past with a vengeance: Theorized reading with diversionary skates on. A high-textual *there* – *Twelfth Night, 1 Henry IV, King Lear* – is admitted to be *there*, all right, in play; but other *theres* are, for these purposes, now granted the real readerly attention. The action has shifted from centre-stage to the wings. It's a shift central to so-called Cultural Studies, of course, in which literary texts take such place as they enjoy as just one more form of signifying practice among the many which comprise any and every culture. In Neo-Historicism – as in some areas of Cultural Studies – the shift can be greatly diverting, in the sense at least of introducing the reader to historical information, to items of interest and amusement in themselves, and sometimes even to things with some enlarging contextual value. But it is, in all seriousness, mainly a diversion. 'The Cultivation of Anxiety: King Lear and His Heirs', the Greenblatt essay about the alleged Baptist King Lear-soundalike is titled. What it represents is a highly cultivated anxiety about the worth of reading any commanding literary text as such.[8]

So: there's the extinction of texts by denial of their real presence; and there's extinction of texts by diverting attention away from them; and then there's extinction by interpretative excess, excess of readerly kindness, the too-heavy readerly embrace that smothers, the too-freely heaped-up load of interpretations that just buries the text it's built on.

To be sure, the fact that strong texts – the timocracy – can stand many reading approaches and will yield to many and various hermeneutic squeezes, is what sustains the classics of literature, keeps them in their front rank as classics. A great part of what defines The Classic is its potential for much rereading.[9] The big ones are indeed copious with meaning, plurivalent, great cornucopiae of hermeneutic possibility, plenipotentious sites of meaning, *grands magasins* for the eager literary shopper. And some foundational assumptions of the linguistic turn are evident responses to and registers of such possibilities for multiplying, proliferating readings. The excited opposition to 'univalence', the revivalistic embrace of 'polysemy', and the endless repetition of Roland Barthes's binary opposition between the merely readable text, the *lisible* one (witness to dull, old-fashioned, unimaginative, inert, closure-besotted reading assumptions and practices) and the lovely and end-lessly rewritable text, the *scriptible* one (open, liberal, gloriously free), which all became staples of critical proclamation and licences for the busy reappropriating of texts in the wake of deconstruction's arrival in the USA: all these were seen, at least in their best light, as registering a proper realization of the reading and rereading potential of great works of literature. (Though some of the temporary excitement, as if reading were now being licensed to enter utterly new territory, was clearly misguided: I don't know anywhere in the whole history of reading where the single monodic meaning, the monovalent text, have been seriously maintained as ideals or achievements, except perhaps among certain upholders of certain sacred texts such as *The Book of Mormon*, among Soviet Realist critics the 1930s, and in the dystopia of Swift's Houyhnhnms in *Gulliver's Travels*, whose nightmare rationality can't cope with verbal ambivalence and obscurity and craves a linguistic purity and perspicacity which reflects Swift's awed derision over Bishop Thomas Sprat's and the young Royal Society's attempts to achieve a 'mathematical plainness of language' – which was doubtless their reac-tion to all those seventeenth-century mystagogues and allegorizers of scripture whose allegorizings had led the charge against Charles the First.) Univalence is another of Theory's throng of straw men.

Theory went too far in its excited glimpsings of a Nietzschean prom-ised land of an endless play of signifiers, an unstoppable heteroglossia. Theory was in many ways ill-served by its twentieth-century prehis-tory among Dadaists and Surrealists, its roots in an aesthetics and lin-guistics which espoused the accidentality of meaning, the pun, the slip of the tongue, and which looked back with favour on Victorian Non-sense writers, and made the monstrously punning *Finnegans Wake* a high model of the modern text. It was ill-served too by so many influential Theorists' family memories of traditional Jewish, rabbinical ways with the texts of the Law and the Prophets, and their attractions to kabbalistic meanings and to midrashic rewritings of biblical story. Theory grew up and flourished in a post-Judaeo-Christian world where the 'confusium of tongues' at the tower of Babel (to quote *Finnegans*

Wake) and the glossalalia of the Christian Day of Pentecost were gladly seized on as models of linguisticity and text. Freud's influential dream text – endlessly proliferating its dark sayings, plunging the interpreter deeper and deeper into the ultimately ungraspable 'dark navel', the *mise en abyme*, of the dream's unplumbable meanings, which owes so much to the rabbinical tradition (*das haben wir behandelt wie einen heiligen Text*: we treated it like a sacred text, was Freud's classic description of his interpretative work) – afforded a current of Theoretical assertion which, after all, came out of the same biblical pot.[10] The Jewish/ Christian Bible's potential for endless rereading, for a perpetuosity of midrash, is what has kept it alive as a classic. But the history of Bible reading is a dangerous precedent when taken as a model for all reading – as it has been, and so influentially, by Bloom and Derrida and Emmanuel Levinas and René Girard and Michel Serres and Walter Benjamin and hosts of others.[11] The rediscovery of the Bible as a potent text by secular literary scholars is, of course, one of Theory's major achievements. But one must tremble a bit as Julian Wolfreys's *Readings* brings forward with characteristic Theorist aplomb Emmanuel Levinas's rabbinical claims about the sacred text's model meanings in his *Beyond the Verse: Talmudic Readings and Lectures* (1994):

> the statement . . . exceeds what it originally wants to say; . . . what it is capable of saying goes beyond what it wants to say; . . . it contains more than it contains; . . . perhaps an inexhaustible surplus of meaning remains locked in the syntactic structures of the sentence, in its word-groups, its actual words, phonemes and letters, in all this materiality of the saying which is potentially signifying all the time. Exegesis would come to free, in these signs, a bewitched significance that smoulders beneath the characters or coils up in all this literature of letters.

An inexhaustible surplus. It's a daunting recipe – as Borges recognized when he worried about Leon Bloy taking the 'absolute text' of holy scripture as a model for all text, all to be read like the Bible text, up and down, sideways, across, numerologically, acrostically. No human being could author such a text; only God could do so; for only 'in the work of a divine mind' is there *nothing* contingent.[12]

Saussure's linguistics, so foundational for Theory, are rooted, and utterly disconcertingly, in his massive effort to expose acrostic-type meanings in European poems, the so-called hypograms, or anagrams. He did give up the attempt at proving these encrypted presences of authors' names, and so on, embedded deep in classical texts – it didn't work – but some Theorists were happy to acclaim the implied vision of a dark valence in writings. Paul de Man praised 'the Saussure of the anagrams' as a pioneer of deconstruction; so did Barbara Johnson. One French critic rhapsodized that the anagrams stood instructively for indeterminate multiplicity and a radical undecidability, the very essence of the deconstructionist vision of text. He forgot that Saussure never actually found enough evidence to prove these hidden meanings actually existed, but the Theorist's need for their presence as 'proof' of radical textual undecidability clearly did exist.[13] There seems little doubt that what helped turn Tzvetan Todorov away from a Saussure-afforced plunge over the cliff of endless heteroglossia was his discovery of Saussure's mystifying faith in glossalalia (Mme Smith, the Geneva medium did, Saussure thought, speak a word or two of Sanskrit, when he was called in to investigate her case; she might even, he thought, have spoken the Martian she claimed!).[14]

With verbal mysteries like these as depth models for language and writing, what price a stop on any reading? And at its most rampant Theory happily eschewed the idea of any interpretative stop. It was just too tempting to slide from Derrida's allegation that texts overflowed all boundaries assigned to them, to believing that nothing could stop you saying (in Frank Kermode's dyspeptic formula) 'absolutely anything you like' about a text.[15]

A useful sense that writings might mean more than one thing, might signify extensively, might resist absolutes of determination or fixity, gave way to such talk as that French anagram enthusiast's about radical undecidability, which soon segued into the idea that nothing could be decided about the meaning of texts. So, on this view, anything goes, and there is no allowed logic or reason why any reading might be wrong. So you'd better get in there and add your new spin to the old heap of readings, however glossalalic. It won't hurt the text. Play the freeplay game. The Polish historian Eva Hoffman has described a onetime Polish Socialist Realist and state film censor who espoused such 'flawless postmodern conclusions': 'I can interpret anything in the way I want. I can make anything mean anything'.[16] An extremely corrupt arts-operator was mouthing a corrupt slogan; but it's one that Theory put about widely, corrupting reading practices no end.

Examples of the corruption are legion, too too numerous for heart's ease. Let Paul Muldoon, a fine Irish poet, but also Professor of Poetry at Oxford, and Howard G. B. Clark Professor in the Humanities at Princeton, serve as an example of making literature mean anything you like, and so killing poems and stories on Theory's licensed premisses. Muldoon's Oxford Clarendon Lectures, *To Ireland, I* is a copious A–Z of Irish writing and imaginings, utterly marred by a kind of zany free associationism – here be floating signifiers if ever you saw them – in which whatever the reader Muldoon wants to perceive as encrypted in a writing is indeed so perceived. Ireland and its writers become a great family tree, joined by odd and tenuous verbal links, the chain-mail of the pun rampant, many of them to do with trees, Irish trees, Irish philological trees. (Ulster was, after all, a Plantation, and English was indeed grafted on to Irish.) Muldoon attends to a story of Elizabeth Bowen's, 'The Tommy Crans'. Crann is Irish for tree. The poet Sir Samuel Ferguson was once described as of 'fine old Presbyterian stock'. John Hewitt is a poet of 'fine old Methodist stock'. In his poetry barbarians fell trees. Ferguson, to whom Hewitt is linked only by a share in Ulster's 'fine old stock', has a poem in which a Fenian had not 'anything / To hide' in Grafton Street, Dublin. Grafton: ah, Graft on! And on Muldoon surges, grafting his meanings onto one another with bracing zest and gratuitous energy. 'The phrase "anything / To hide" brings me neatly to the case of Douglas Hyde (1860–1949)'. Hyde wrote an essay 'On the Necessity for De-Anglicizing Ireland'. He talked about the Young Ireland poets trying to give Ireland a new literature in English. 'It was a most brilliant effort, but the old bark had been too recently stripped off the Irish tree, and the trunk could not take as it might have done to a fresh one.' So Hyde. 'We recognize', says Muldoon, 'Hyde's grafting metaphor, though it seems a little confused here in terms of whether it's "trunk" or "slip" that "takes".' Seems? It certainly does seem a little confused. And, I'd say, it seems pretty clear that Hyde is confusing grafting (adding something to an old tree trunk) and the production of cork, where the old bark is stripped off the cork-tree and new bark grows to replace it. Certainly you don't 'strip' old bark off prior to making a graft. But Muldoon will have his grafting-on. And on and on he goes, grafting his new meanings onto old poems and stories. In Lady Gregory's *Gods and Fighting Men*:

> 'Diarmuid stood up on a high bough of the boughs of the tree, and he rose with a light leap by the shaft of his spear, and lit on the grass far beyond Finn and the Fianna'. This appears in [James Joyce's story] 'The Dead' as the '*light* from the street lamp' that 'lay in a long *shaft*' that Gabriel/Diarmuid points out to Gretta/ Grainne, who avails herself of this very mode of transport when she's in the Gresham Hotel:
>
> > She turned away from the mirror slowly *and walked along the shaft of light* towards him.[17]

Daftness, all this. It's a shafting of texts with a vengeance. 'Conglome-writing' is Muldoon's label for these alleged shuntings and allusions of Joyce. Well, as criticism this is *conglomereading*. It has a crazy plausibility – but a plausibility only reminiscent of the worst excesses of the pre-Theory guessworking that used to go on in the footnotes of editions of Shakespeare and the like, and which Theory's new Anything Goes licensing laws have revived and sanctioned. Nobody got up and expostulated, during Muldoon's lectures, against his freehand slathering of texts in such free associationism because, I guess, audiences are only too used to modern reading under Theory's standard as wilful rewriting. Such interpreting 'says no more, no less, than that language has no "proper" meaning': that's Geoffrey Hartman's enthusiastic take on such writing (and Hartman became one of the linguistic turn's wildest hebraising improvisers of deconstructionist readings). Much to the point is that Muldoon is not an obviously card-carrying Theorist. What his excessive way of reading indicates is how what Hartman calls the 'in-difference' of deconstruction's allegations – its raging programme of pursuing irresolubility – has travelled into the ordinary reading practices of our time. Its product is indeed indifferent reading. And even Hartman had his occasional worries about what he calls the "'plurisy" of verbal play that "dies in its own too much"' – *plurisy*, one spelling of *pleurisy*, a condition that takes your breath away, as such displays of random virtuosity as Muldoon's (and Hartman's) can do, but which is also killing you off.[18]

In the Cambridge University reading experiments I. A. Richards reported in his *Practical Criticism* (1929), his students' making of 'private poems' out of the ones in front of them was a frequent offence. Too many bright readers, equipped with a detective's imagination, were, simply, not reading, but producing meanings which 'are not given in the poem', which 'reflect only the reader's own private attempt at an analogous poem constructed on the basis . . . of this poem's apparent subject-matter'. 'It would seem that a dense medium of the reader's own poetic product – "much embryo, much abortion" – surrounds him and intervenes very often to prevent communication with the poet.'[19] Richards's confidence that some readings can be ruled out, and that others must be ruled in, sounds distinctly old-fashioned, startling even – so far has Theory occupied the main critical ground.

What is wrong with the making of private poems, the paid-up Theorist asks: isn't that a true reading act? Happily not everyone agrees. Umberto Eco is powerfully hostile to what he calls *over-interpretation* (and I agree with him strongly). 'I accept the statement that a text can have many senses. I refuse the statement that a text can have every sense.' (He's refusing Richard Rorty's statements to that effect.) '*It is not true that everything goes.*' Acting as if it did is a kind of paranoia. There are '*impossible pertinences*' (some readings will be wrong); and also '*crazy pertinences*' (think Muldoon . . .). If all interpreters are right, then all of them, says Eco, are wrong.[20] To think otherwise is to endorse what Gerard Graff has called the 'weightlessness' of talk in the Humanities (and he means Theory, means what happens when 'we see poets and critics as licensed to say anything they please'; means what René Wellek meant when he accused US Theorists of 'philosophising on their own').[21]

Even Jacques Lacan, that canny, even if sometimes wild analyst, knew that not all analyses were valid – and in the extremely un-weight-less world of psychoanalysis, where real patients have real needs for real answers, how could that not be? 'Interpretation is not open to all meanings.' And Lacan rebuked anyone who would invoke the arbitrary 'connection of a signifier to a signifier in dreams': free play of signifiers, signifiers without fixed signifieds.

> This would be to concede to those who rise up against the character of uncertainty in analytic interpretation that, in effect, all interpretations are possible, which is patently absurd. The fact that I have said that the effect of interpretation is to isolate in the subject a kernel, a *kern*, to use Freud's own term, of *non-sense*, does not mean that interpretation is in itself nonsense.[22]

And so forth. But you don't hear this caveat repeated very much among our Theorists. One of the features of the Theory era has been that Theorists pick and choose what they would hear from their gurus. Jacques Derrida has complained endlessly about this tendency to selective attention. Once they're installed, what I. A. Richards called *stock notions* – and the idea that 'anything goes' because Derrida, or whoever, says so is one of the most persistent stock notions of Theory – stay firmly in place even when denied by those masters believed to uphold them. What I shall end up praising as readerly *tact* would not only respect the integrity of literary texts and attempt none of the disappearing tricks I've talked about in this chapter, by letting literary texts speak in their own voice, but would also mean listening to what *Theorists* really say as well.

7

Textual Abuse: Or, Down With Stock Responses

J. LACAN. One wants to be loved for everything – not only for one's ego, as Descartes says, but for the colour of one's hair, for one's idiosyncrasies, for one's weaknesses, for everything.
O. MANNONE. *It was Pascal who said that, not Descartes.*
J. LACAN. There is a passage in Descartes on the progressive purification of the ego beyond all its specific qualities. But you aren't wrong, in so far as Pascal tries to take us beyond the creature.
O. MANNONE. *He said it explicitly.*

The Seminar of Jacques Lacan, Book I,
Freud's Papers on Technique 1953–1954

On 15 May 2001 I receive a cast-your-bread-on-the-waters email from a High School student in the USA. She seeks advice on an essay set on *Wuthering Heights*. Her class is to look for evidence of incest in that novel. There is no incest in *Wuthering Heights*. Thinking there might be some comes from a fashionable notion that there must be some in every family; it's what current therapy, false-memory syndrome, and so on, endorse; and those children in Emily Brontë's novel, they're so close, and their families are so dysfunctional. . . . Sexual abuse is on teacher's mind, on teacher's agenda, in teacher's ideology of family life, and, because of certain Theorized literary practice, which has gone in a lot for what a recent Queer Studies tome has called *Sex*

Scandal: The Private Parts of Victorian Fiction,[1] incest has evidently sprung to teacher's mind as a possibility in *Wuthering Heights.* Teacher probably got the idea in the first place from some college teacher of his/hers. It's a suggested reading lifted without much thought straight off the Theory shelf, a notion from Theory stock, producing a stock response, as dismissively described by I. A. Richards in *Practical Criticism*: 'views and emotions already fully prepared in the reader's mind. . . . The button is pressed, and then the author's work is done, for immediately the record starts playing in quasi- (or total) independence of the poem which is supposed to be its origin or instrument'. And stock responses are bad readings, as Richards's *Practical Criticism* repeatedly demonstrates. Textual abuse follows – as in this case – when some stock notion leads the reading effort.

And Theory has stacked the critical shelves with what have become direly stock notions: with prejudices, prejudgements, which turn into prejudiced readings. Misreading across the ages has no doubt often been driven by fixed ideas about what might be in texts, and bad reading in any age can often be defined as simply getting out of a text what you looked for without enough reference to what was actually in it. (You see, of course, that I assume there are things actually in a text.) If ideology is, classically, false consciousness; which is, again classically, false epistemology, and encourages, classically, false hermeneutics; then ideologies of reading, and ideology- or Theory-driven reading will be no less guilty of such interpretative errings. Ideologies of reading have always existed; they're even, as I've suggested, inevitable to readers and reading. But in our Theory times they have so multiplied, are so very numerous, with the inevitable consequence of far more reading distortion than ever before. And, quite clearly, Theorists do misread, and on a spectacular scale. Theory-inspired readers go awry with terrible regularity. Theory, quite evidently, distorts reading. Theory does violence to the meanings of texts. Theory's reading record is, simply, bad. Theorists provide endless bad examples of textual handling.

I suppose it's no accident hereabouts that so many of Theory's masterminds have not been in any recognized sense literary critics, and certainly not in any normal way literary historians. They read a lot, of course: Marx and Freud, Lacan and Derrida and Foucault; and what they do is commonly heralded as reading and rereading ('Lacan reads Freud', etc.).[2] But their hermeneutical business is often not directed primarily at understanding literary texts, not even the literariness of the literary texts that they happen to be discussing. Marx on *Robinson Crusoe*, Freud on E. T. A. Hoffmann, Derrida on Joyce or Kafka, Lacan on *Hamlet* or Poe's *The Purloined Letter*, are all, in literary critical terms, incidental readings, readings done primarily to illustrate the role of such texts in the greater narrative of socialism, psychoanalysis, deconstruction, or whatever. These are symptomatic rather than particular readings. That's how texts function in the scene of reading commanded by what Quentin Skinner has labelled Grand Theory.[3] The Theoretical keeps looking way beyond the textual particular. No wonder particularity suffers. And this heedlessness – or this heeding differently – sets a terribly bad example to people whose prime business is reading. It's a bad example reinforced by doctrines – to some extent, by the whole doctrine – promoting a sort of heedlessness as a principle for reading.

On principle Theory encourages the reader to vamp away to her/his heart's content in the text's lovely abundant empty spaces, its fissures and lacks, in what Roland Barthes has called the 'triumphant plurality' of the text, where interpretation is not 'giving it a meaning', but 'on the contrary appreciating whatever it's made of'.[4] This is to vamp in the sense of that old instruction on popular music scores, 'Vamp til ready', as well as in Gilbert and Gubar's sense of the woman reader as *femme fatale* or vamp, woman without patriarchal bounds, projecting boundless female desires into the infixity of the text.[5] Which is another way of saying: Abuse the text to your own satisfaction; enjoy yourself at the text's expense. Textual abuse. Quite in keeping with Harold Bloom's influential vision of reading and literary history as a necessary mis-taking process. Notoriously, he envisions young poets achieving their own voice only by wrestling violently with the strong father-predecessors, wrenching their words, mis-prizing them harshly. All reading is, then, abusive. A *traductio abusive*: thus Philip

Lewis, warmly endorsed by Cynthia Chase, who praises 'the strategy of a rigorously abusive translation' among the Romantic poets. Rigorous abuse. An ethic, then, of abuse. Professor Chase was brought up critically, of course, by Paul de Man, for whom all figuring, writing, poetry, and all figuring-out of texts, was disfigurement and defacing. For his part, Harold Bloom models all meaning on that strange kabbalistic moment, to which I've already referred, the mythic Breaking of the Vessels. Derrida takes the story of Moses breaking the Tablets of the Law as one great emblem of how meaning arrives. Roland Barthes's metaphors for what analysis does with texts include *écartant*, spreading it out; but also *brisant*, smashing it up, shattering it, splintering it, breaking it in bits.[6] The Theory era saw the resurrection of *katachresis*, the Greek rhetorical figure of poetic abuse – always translated in the Latin rhetoric books as *abusio* – as absolutely central to all poetic activity, and to what readings would detect in texts, alongside the more benign metaphor and metonymy. Theory went in overtly for catachretical reading.

Some catachresis is normal. Ancient rhetoricians thought so, and the modern centrality Theory granted catachresis is evidently derived from Greek and Roman thought about the rhetoricity of poetry, about what poeticity might consist of. Poetry makes mistakes, language is fallible, and so, inevitably, are readers and readings. Even Homer nods. Ezra Pound once sneered that no professor of literature was ever sacked for ignorance. Ignorance is natural, if deplorable. The whole world of English-speaking criticism, for example, from Hillis Miller to Homi Bhabha and beyond, seems to think not only that there's a great (and analytically useful) binary opposition between the uncanny and the canny, the unhomely and the homely, but that it is to be expressed with all the authority of Freud's German, in his essay on 'The Uncanny', as the *unheimlich* and the *heimlich*. It's an opposition as useful to structuralism and deconstruction (Hillis Miller rather brilliantly deconstructs it in his famous article 'The Critic as Host') as it is to postcolonial studies.[7] But nice as it is to have the rhyming pair *heimlich/ unheimlich*, so attractive to so many analyses (every undergraduate essay likes and uses it), it is in fact based on the mistaken assumption that

German still has the extant operative word *heimlich* as the opposite of *unheimlich*. And it doesn't: the opposite of *unheimlich* is *heimelig*. *Heimelig* appears in Freud's essay, but it doesn't rhyme so well with *unheimlich*. The mistaken assumption about the modernity of *heimlich* comes about, I observe, because the publishers of James Strachey's Standard English translation, not wishing to bore readers and wanting to save space, left out Freud's long excursion into German lexicons which makes the mere historicity of *heimlich* clear. For English readers of Freud's essay the mistake is understandable (I made it myself, until alerted by a German student). Something was lost in the translation. But the *traductio abusive*, the mis-taking of Freud's essay, is not deliberate. Which cannot be said for Paul de Man.

With de Man abusive translation is not just normal, it's quite deliberate and evidently driven by the interests of Theory. Central to de Man's principles of reading is the idea that every aspect of reading, of textuality, involves translation. Translation stands for everything the critic and the critical enterprise are about. Translation for de Man is the great metaphor for, and the exemplary case of, philosophy, history, rhetoricity, Theory. Translation = metaphoricity, *metaphorein* in Greek, *translatio* in Latin. And translation according to de Man is not possible – like all writing it's a stymied activity, aporetic, abysmal, and so on. Its impossibility registers all the negative capabilities Theory is aware and capable of. And the illustration of this, the authority for it? It's Walter Benjamin's famous essay 'The Task of the Translator', *Die Aufgabe des Übersetzers*. De Man focuses on the word *Aufgabe*.

> *Aufgabe*, task, can also mean the one who has to give up. If you enter the Tour de France and you give up, that is the *Aufgabe* – 'er hat aufgegeben', he doesn't continue in the race any more. It is in that sense also the defeat, the giving up of the translator. The translator has to give up in relation to the task of refinding what was there in the original.[8]

These were de Man's last words, his last lecture, in 1983. They came with all his great critical authority, the authority too of his heavily

91

European-accented English. (If anybody in Yale should know something about German, this, his accent declared, was he.) But he was simply lying about *Aufgabe*, abusing his authoritative position to mislead his audience. German *Aufgabe* – task, exercise, homework – is not to be confused with the verb *aufgeben* in the sense of abandon, 'give up'. It means that which you give up only in the sense of handing the finished job up to, or over to, the person who commanded you to perform it. There is no sense at all in *Aufgabe* of 'the task you have to abandon' (let a German school-student tell the teacher she hasn't completed her homework tasks, the *Aufgaben*, and won't be handing them over, won't give them in to teacher, because *Aufgabe* is a self-contradicting, self-deconstructing, aporetic word, cancelling itself out from the start, and see what happens). De Man was making it up, faking it, knowingly misleading – driven by Theory's *parti pris*, by prejudice, to get in a stock response. Nowhere in his essay does Benjamin say the task of the translator is impossible – only that it is very hard (at best it can only be like an interlinear version of the Bible, but it can be done in this fashion). And such mistaking on Theory-driven grounds is typical of Paul de Man.[9] It's all too typical of other paid-up Theorists, as well. In his much reprinted 'Letter to a Japanese Friend', which dwells on the great difficulties of translation, particularly of the word *deconstruction*, Derrida refers in shorthand fashion to Benjamin: '"the impossible task of the translator" (Benjamin)'.[10] He can't have read Benjamin's essay himself, or recently, and is clearly only reporting de Man's traducing exposition of it. How misreading spawns misreading in the school of Theory!

The fault lies with dogmatism itself. That dogma infects the readerly vision, corrupts the readerly touch, has long been recognized. I. A. Richards's Practical Critical experiments repeatedly showed doctrinalists, Christians, atheists, socialists in the main, unable to read the poem in front of them, being held back, or distracted, even blinded, because of 'Doctrinal Adhesions' as Richards labelled them. 'Another troublesome problem' he called this: somewhere between Stock Responses and *general critical preconceptions* (prior demands made upon poetry as a result of theories – conscious or unconscious – about its

nature and value)'. Critical preconceptions, he says, 'intervene endlessly, as the history of criticism shows only too well, between the
reader and the poem'.[11] Richards's nice metaphor for the reader bound
by theoretical preconceptions is that this is like being on an 'unlucky'
diet, which prevents you from eating something you are 'starving
for', 'even when it is at [your] very lips'. And Richards's most terrify-
ing case of a reader led astray by dogmas of theorized prejudgement is
Tolstoy, who in his *What is Art?* (translated by Aylmer Maude, 1899)
purged European writing of anything which did 'not directly urge the
union of men, or whose appeal is suspected to be limited to cultured
and aristocratic circles'. Out went Shakespeare and Dante and Goethe,
at the expense of *Adam Bede* and *Uncle Tom's Cabin*. 'Blinded by the
light of a retarded conversion . . . forgetting in the fierceness of his
new convictions all the experience that had in earlier years made up
his own creations, he flung himself, a Principle in each hand, upon
the whole host of European masterpieces and left as he believed hardly
a survivor standing.'[12]

You can sympathize, to a degree, perhaps, with the doctrinalists'
misery that the world and text don't always go their way. You can
certainly smell the doctrinalists' fear about any resistance of phenomena to their lines of thinking. And you can understand why their
desire for texts especially to go a particular way might lead to some
bending and twisting, to textual bruising and abusing – some of it no
doubt unconscious, sincere even. I mean, I don't at all doubt the
sincerity of Philip Larkin, say, when in a tough attack on the 'American' idea that 'all poems come from other poems', he invoked 'the
poet' who said that 'every man is an island' (when John Donne famously said that 'no man is an island'), nor that of Harold Bloom when
he rewrites the end of Dostoevsky's *Crime and Punishment* and has
Raskolnikov the murderer repent 'truly at last, in the novel's uncon-
vincing epilogue, when he surrenders wholly to the Magdalene-like
Sonya, as the hope for his Lazarus-ascension from death to salvation' –
which is a very strong overstatement. The epilogue states very clearly
that Raskolnikov does not even open the copy of the New Testament Sonya Marmeladov gave him to take into Siberia, the book

from which she read the story of Lazarus's raising from the dead, but to no avail, certainly at the time, with the murderer. (And it's a question of resurrection, by the way, not ascension from the dead.) Mistaking of this ending is not uncommon (Julia Kristeva shares it in her book *The Black Sun*: Raskolnikov plunges, she wrongly thinks, 'into the reading of Lazarus's story from the New Testament that Sonia lent him').[13] It's more than a bit rich that Bloom's erring should come in a book entitled *How To Read and Why*.[14] But sincere or not, such misreadings are still maltreatments, less creative misreadings than simply uncreating ones and they're miscreations driven, certainly in the case of Larkin and Bloom, by dogma – Larkin's anti-intertextualism so strong he rewrites almost the most famous line of Donne to uphold it; Bloom's hostility to Christian endings so passionate that he invents one in order to deplore its failure of conviction. In Bloom's case a misreading arising from a particular dogmatic disposition comes endorsed by his well-advertised principle of misreading as necessary to reading and to the course of literary history. Not unlike Richard Rorty, in fact, who thinks there is no 'fact' beyond language and deliberately misappropriates a Larkin poem about death ('And once you have walked the length of your mind'), suggesting it is about the fear not of death but rather of not being an innovative poet – which is a purely linguistic fear, and so proves Rorty's declared stand of principle about mere linguisticity.[15]

And dogma does this, does it all the time, does it too often for these kinds of results to be accidental. Nothing 'in the recent history of aesthetic opinion', thought Richards, was 'so remarkable' as Tolstoy's dogmatic onslaught on the arts. But devastating Theory-driven misjudgements reminiscent altogether of Tolstoy's became simply normal in the Theory era. Only a Theorist who confuses a liking for jest with the stricter necessities of historical and semantic truth, would outrageously suggest, as Terry Eagleton does in his book on Shakespeare, that 'There is some evidence that the word "nothing" in Elizabethan English meant the female genitals', when this is patently not the case. Hamlet may sneer hurtfully to Ophelia before the play-scene about woman as *naught*, and a *nothing*, and thus pun crudely on her

vagina as well as referring in a standard Elizabethan way to her noth-
ingness, her blankness as a female. But this is metaphor; the noun
nothing by no means *meant* vagina.[16] Only a theorist who nailed his
colours so hard to a Theoretical mast which made his name, so that
changing his line would amount to having to say sorry, would play
the bizarrely distortive game Stanley Fish does with the opening words
of Milton's 'Lycidas', 'Yet once more' – ringing the changes on mainly
far-fetched – in fact far-dragged – possibilities (the only one holding
water being the suggestion of the poet's weary sadness at having to
commemorate the dead yet again), and working in a really quite irrelevant discussion of the Letter to the Hebrews which uses those three
words, and all in order to prove how smart readers like him do this
sort of thing because they know this is a poem and that's what poetry
readings require. So yet once more Stanley Fish proves that the words
of a poem count for far less than the Theory a Theorist brings to
them: a prejudiced business only made worse by Fish knowing exactly what trick he's working and proud of it ('I could go on for ever
in this vein – I haven't been a Miltonist these thirty years for nothing').[17] And only desperate Theorists, rocked by the news of Paul de
Man's anti-semitic writings and early Fascist sympathies, would seek
to rescue their friend and mentor from obliquity as Derrida and Barbara
Johnson and Shoshana Felman and others did, by carefully misreading
those texts to suggest that anti-semitism was in some deconstructive
way really pro-Jewishness, or not saying what it really said, as well as
by declaring that anyway reference and history didn't matter, as the
master had clearly laid down.[18] But such misappropriation is sadly
normal among Theorists. So normal that just a few examples will have
to suffice.

When in *Das Kapital*, out of hostility to religion, Marx claims that
the 'prayers and the like' in *Robinson Crusoe* need not be taken into
account because they are sources of mere recreation and pleasure and
that it is the novel's demonstration of a capitalist *homo economicus* at
work that's the only serious truth of that fiction, bang goes one great
dimension of Defoe's novel, the keen religious, Protestant side of
the founding of the English novel, and the reinforcing of Western

bourgeois selfhood in that strange meeting Defoe arranges between religion and the rise of capitalism.[19] Marx's casual party preference, his stock response, thus perverts a novel, perverts a whole history of the novel, and perverts any true grasp of a piece of writing and a whole context of that writing. And Theory's politics are often to blame like this.

Edward Said, for instance, earnestly corrupts and slants Joseph Conrad's African story *Heart of Darkness* in pursuit of his postcolonialist analyses in his *Culture and Imperialism* (1993). He's following hard, of course, in the footsteps of the novelist Chinua Achebe, whose crude distorting of Conrad's great anti-imperialist fiction, accusing it of being sunk into the very racism and colonialism it deplores throughout, has become quite a canonical critical account within postcolonialist studies. Simply, Achebe can't read this novel straight, being blinkered by his belief that Conrad is a vulgar racist, myth-maker-in-chief to British colonial interests, whose writing is dehumanizing its African subjects. Prejudgement is occluding this fiction almost absolutely from Achebe. And presumably also from all those readers who profess admiration for Achebe's now extremely standard piece.[20] Edward Said is, happily, cannier. He grants that Conrad 'was very critical of Belgian colonialism'. But still his fiction is caught up in the 'scramble for Africa' and implicated in the ideologies of modern imperialism. So Said is still out to get Conrad, especially his justification of 'us' as colonists in contrast with the Romans. He objects to Conrad's idea that 'our' efficiency *saves* us, and that we are *redeemed* by an 'idea'. This contrast is 'oddly perceptive', Said thinks; it illuminates 'the special mix of power, ideological energy, and practical attitude characterizing European imperialism'. But Said is rather imperceptive, I think, about it. He glosses the first as an openly aggressive matter, utterly clear about the colonists' 'power to take over territory', and the second as more of a cover-up, an attempt to disguise the aggression of the first with a self-justificatory and morally aggrandizing plea. And the 'redemption', Said thinks, is 'a step in a sense beyond salvation'. But in what sense? In the Christian discourses Conrad draws these terms from, those are parallel and analogous terms, they mean precisely the same as each other; there is no possible sense of progress from one to the other. Conrad is offering a parallel set of justifications, not a contrastive one. Said is getting it quite wrong, is simply not hearing Conrad. And, I suggest, it's because his ideological predisposition is pointing him forcefully in the Achebe direction that he is just not grasping what Conrad says about that redemptive 'idea'. 'An idea at the back of it; not a sentimental pretence but an idea; and an unselfish belief in the idea – something you can set up, and bow down before, and offer sacrifice to.' In other words this 'idea' is, in Christian terms – in biblical terms, in terms of the discourses in which *salvation* and *redemption* have their source – a false god, an idol, a fetish, a graven image of the sort the Ten Commandments forbid Yahweh's followers from making as an object of worship. The white men with their 'idea' are only on a par with the Africans they are subjugating who, of course, 'bow down to wood and stone', and haven't got the white world's Christian pretensions. So Conrad is being savagely critical of a Christian world turning away from true religion to worship the false god of the imperialist idea – and using Christian language, salvation, redemption, as they do so. The text is clear enough, but Said's over-eagerness for villains in his (important) inspections of the close links between empire and the 'European novel as we know it' is simply preventing him from reading that clarity.[21]

Sniffing out racist tendencies tends to have distortive effects. Taking offence on theorized ground can be the glibbest of stock responses. Even Virginia Woolf's *A Room Of One's Own*, her great polemic against patriarchy and, yes, male racism, can be read as racist and hostile to black women to boot, if read through the scratchy lens of Theory. So we find Catharine Stimpson, a lively feminist literary-historian, greatly mistaking Woolf's sharp rebuttal of the appropriating gaze of the English male colonizer. Admittedly, Woolf's 'very fine Negress' can give the reader a jolt when she pops up at the end of a violently angry sentence about men wanting and marking and cutting and taking everything they see. Women, says Woolf, furiously,

are not even now as concerned about the health of their fame as men are, and, speaking generally, will pass a tombstone or a

97

signpost without feeling an irresistible desire to cut their names on it, as Alf, Bert or Chas. must do in obedience to their instinct, which murmurs if it sees a fine woman go by, or even a dog, Ce chien est à moi. And of course it may not be a dog, I thought, remembering Parliament Square [in London], the Sieges Allee [in Berlin] and other avenues [where imperialist campaigns are celebrated]; it may be a piece of land or a man with curly black hair. It is one of the great advantages of being a woman that one can pass even a very fine negress without wishing to make an Englishwoman of her.

According to Stimpson, this is feminist criticism 'infiltrated' by racism. 'Carelessly, cruelly, the [last] sentence ruptures "woman" from "Negress", granting "woman" subjectivity and "negress", no matter how fine, mere objecthood.' But the only cruelty around is in Stimpson's prickly carelessness about siting the negress in the context of Woolf's text. Stimpson can't read, can't attend to irony, let alone to irony's stronger-mouthed sister, sarcasm. She's simply not seeing Woolf's run of thought from the male takers of fine women, land and black men (men 'with curly black hair') to their female contrastive opposites who do not wish to colonize anybody, including black African women, even beautiful ones. Woolf's contempt is the more, given her lesbianism: she, clearly, did often fancy 'fine women', perhaps even 'fine' negresses; but she disclaims the male colonizers' assumption that you may take, you may rape, whatever you fancy, just because you fancy it. As for that bit of Theory lingo about syntactic and semantic *rupture*, I'm surprised Stimpson didn't dwell on the syntactic link between *woman* and *dog*. But perhaps even Stimpson could hear the heavy irony there and wouldn't dare to broach the idea of a feminist criticism 'infiltrated' by a bestializing view of woman. But the woman–dog sentence might at least have brought home to the critic that just because items lie next to each other in a sentence you can't jump to conclusions about how they're related to, or indeed 'ruptured' from, each other. But this spurring of interpretation by the scorpions of ideology is, alas, all too common.[22]

When sexual politics is in the driving seat, the critical vehicle is too often all over the road. My emailing high-school inquirer's teacher has nothing, one might say, on Eve Kosofsky Sedgwick. Nor, for that matter, on *Sex Scandal: The Private Parts of Victorian Fiction* (1996*)* by William A. Cohen. Cohen's freeplaying romp across the canon of Victorian writing comes with Kosofsky Sedgwick's backing – it's in the Duke University Press's Series Q, whose editors include her and Jonathan Goldberg. Parts of it appeared earlier in reputed Theory-infected journals across the USA, as well as in Duke's *Displacing Homophobia: Gay Male Perspective in Literature and Culture* (1989). So this is out of pukka Theory territory, and, with a certain symptomaticity, I'm afraid, it is by and large appalling tosh.

Cohen follows the lead of Foucault's *History of Sexuality* (1976 in French, 1981 in English) in having the Victorians very over-sexed. In a glorious hermeneutic helter-skelter of over-reading, sanctioned by Freud's way with dream-work and by linguistic-turners with psychoanalysis on their minds, such as the linguist Roman Jakobson, nothing in the novels Cohen analyses is allowed to be itself, not to be allegorical, not to ricochet along a glorious signifying chain where associations and substitutions, metaphors and metonymies, turn into each other and over each other, turn and turn about, all at the interpreter's will, all with a dizzying arbitrariness. In his chapter on 'Trollope's Trollop', Cohen's reading of *The Eustace Diamonds* (1873), the jewel-box containing the diamonds which are the centre of that novel's family squabbles and legal contentions, is of course 'over-determined'. It is the bad-girl heroine Lizzie's pudenda ('According to an elementary substitutive logic'), which is, after Freud's famous way with Dora's reticule = vagina reading, merely par for this course. But then, oddly, the stones it contains are also to be read as testicles. This is because they're 'the family jewels', which 'designate the supposedly scarce resource of reproductive male sexuality, materialized in the seat of spermatic production: the testes'. Well, maybe – though English readers will be relieved that Cohen appears never to have heard of the British slang term 'family jewels' for the whole male genitalia. But for all that, in real life, testicles never get into the female jewel box, unless by some freakish physicality even Michel Foucault would find it hard to credit. And even were they to do that, they would never be *stored up* in vaginas. Lizzie's jewel-box is where the stones are stored.

But then balls are, we might say, balls, especially in what is such a critical balls-up as this. When one of Lizzie's suitors, the caddish Lord George de Bruce Carruthers, turns against her, complaining at some metaphoric length that she's using him in her efforts to retain the valuable 'paraphernalia' – the 'swag' is the kernel of a nut he had troubled to crack; he has now been left only with 'the shell'; she got the kernel; now she finds that she can't 'eat' it by herself she's returning to him for help – it's no surprise to find Cohen equating these metaphors with the jewels/testicles. He's enticed no doubt by the still current slangy metonym of *nuts* for testicles. But Carruthers is actually metaphoricizing the jewels as the *kernel* of a nut, not as nuts *per se*. And of course Cohen has no thoughts on cracked shells. He just leaves out any inconvenient bits of text in his nutty reading.

And he's quite blatant about the way he's playing his metaphoric game according to private rules. Had enough of nuts = testicles? Just move on, then – 'such symbolic suggestions can sustain a literary interest only so long as they resist becoming ossified'. So the reader is to pop in and out of the 'symbolic register', as she wills. We are to note the way 'The jewels' metaphoric relation to male sexuality . . . slides . . . into a metonymic representation of female sexuality as well.' As well? One of the policemen investigating the jewels' disappearance thinks Lizzie might have them 'tied about her person' – which, according to Cohen, is a 'metonymic rubbing up against her body' which 'also signifies sexually'. But signifies what exactly, by this stage of the reading? Are they still the vagina and/or the testicles? The keys to the box are in a bag 'tied round' Lizzie's neck. So they're 'touching her skin', says Cohen in his ready glossing way. Well, no, the keys are not touching her skin, they're in a bag that does that. And were the jewels to be 'tied about her person' they would presumably be in a bag too – pressing on her body, you might think, but hardly, as Cohen has it, 'rubbing up against her body' – doing a bit of sexual frotting. Rubbing up is a nice thought, but pure fantasy. But in any case the policeman is simply speculating, as Cohen is. But how! Cohen is making it all up as he goes along – drawing on a whole Theory history of psychoanalytic allegorizing going all the way back to Freud's happily sexualized reading of dream-text substitutions. He is, what's more, guaranteeing his speculations by the good old Freudian repression argument. The more unprovable the reading, the more obvious it must be because that is how repression always works. And since Cohen is also offering the bluffer's guide to the repressiveness of the Victorians, then there must be, there always will be, repressions in Victorian writing. Which means a licence to find what you will sexually, and to read sexually exactly how you wish.

Masturbation, now. That was, we know, a large Victorian anxiety; so that must be a large repressed item, and one easy to uncover, especially if you come armed with your boy-scout repression-meter-reader's badge. So: 'In the masturbator's guide to the English novel, at least under the heading "men's bodies", Charles Dickens would doubtless merit a good deal of attention'. And why? Because of his obvious repression of the term and its activity, which is making him make do with obvious substitutes for it in his fictions. Charlie Bates in *Oliver Twist* is occasionally referred to as Master Bates. Master Bates, eh? But that 'pun' is probably just a coincidence, too obvious. When, though, he's called Master Charles Bates, 'we are guaranteed to continue imagining' the pun – 'like the onanist, always fantasizing about what is not at hand in order to keep aroused what is'. Which is a lot like saying that although the characters Master Bates and Seaman Stains and Roger the cabin-boy do not actually show up in John Ryan's famous British kiddy books about the pirate Captain Pugwash and his crew – though 'every schoolboy knows' they do – their presence is somehow guaranteed by the constant presence in the stories of the hero Tom the cabin-boy. Tom: it might as well be Roger mightn't it? Ryan really wants Roger, surely? Rogering cabin-boys is, we all know, what went on and goes on aboard ship; and isn't that how Seaman Stains arrived in the playground imagination? When in Fagin's thieves' kitchen Dickens's 'Master Bates' produces 'four pocket handkerchiefs' and calls them 'wipes', ancient slang for handkerchiefs, Cohen knows exactly how to read them. They're 'the gear for cleaning whatever mess his name might imply'. Actually, Fagin's gang make their living by washing the stolen wipes and taking them around the corner to sell them to the Jewish second-hand clothes merchants in Monmouth Street. They would not want to mess up their carefully washed hand-kerchiefs again, once they'd gone to the bother of washing them. Cohen is turning *Oliver Twist* into *Portnoy's Complaint*, a novel Dickens hasn't written, but which Cohen wishes he had, and thinks that Dickens wishes he had. The critic is in effect wiping out *Oliver Twist* in a perverse reading of the wipes. Cohen's reading alone is making a mess.

But then any word, any object, is up for tactless grabs in this interpretative free-for-all once the Theorist has got the bit between his teeth. Fagin's boys quiz Oliver. Does he know what a *prig* is? Oliver does, but being polite and not wanting to offend his new friends, he stops himself from quite saying *thief*. 'It's a th——', he says, and then stops. The Artful Dodger, looking at Master Bates, admits that *he* is a 'th——', and proud of it, and then he gives 'his hat a furious cock'. *Prig*, which indeed meant *thief*, is, Cohen solemnly tells us with a pseudo-learned glance at the regular Germanic languages' 'detour' between p's and f's, really to be taken as *frig*: 'Victorian slang for manual stimulation of the genitals'. That is true of *frig*, but a *prig* remains a *prig*; it is not a *frig* (as well declare that *pig* can be read as *fig* whenever you fancy it). And in any case a *frig* was an act, not a person committing the act: *he* was a *frigger*. But then there's that 'ferocious cock'. A penis, thinks Cohen. Well, a cock can indeed be a penis, and on Cohen's reckoning it must always mean or hint that, even if, as here, it merely purports the angle of a hat on a head. I fail myself to imagine anyone turning his hat into a *furious penis* or, trickier still, *giving* his hat a furious penis. This is reading as verbal rot, a late result of letting signifier freeplay come in as an allowable idea, and then allowing it to settle down among us. And, yet once more, all this verbal pat-ball comes undergirded by the repression = truth hypothesis: masturbation was scandalous, unspeakable, therefore it was repressed, and so 'even in the absence' of explicit references to it we

have to assume its presence. This process of erotic meanings generated especially in their repression is for Cohen the very essence of
Victorian literariness. But pointing it all out is, in fact, only what
Byron accused Keats of, namely 'frigging the imagination' – and frigging
about as well with poetics, with definitions of the literary, let alone
with definitions of Victorian literariness.

But once started, this particular reading hand-job can't stop. In
Great Expectations Dickens 'raises the issue of masturbation by referring to it [yet again] in such a way as to announce the impossibility of
articulating it as such'. The small boy Pip steals a slice of bread and
butter for the starving convict Magwitch. He thus becomes a prig, a
thief. He's so burdened by a guilty conscience about the theft, his
'secret burden' of guilt, that he hides the piece of bread and butter
down his trousers. This becomes 'the secret burden down the leg'.
He's terribly afraid it will fall out of the bottom of his trousers as he
stands stirring his step-sister's Christmas pudding. It is 'the load upon
my leg', reminding him constantly of Magwitch's fettered ankles, the
load upon *his* leg. Cohen seizes avidly on the guilty burden, or load,
down the trouser as a register of Pip's masturbatory guilt: what every
'male adolescent' feels. Phonemic ambiguity (prig: frig) becomes semantic and ethical: guilty slice of bread and butter: hard-on; butter:
ejaculate. The burden is happily disposed of when Pip 'slipped away
and deposited that part of my conscience in my garret bedroom'. Pip
is a little Portnoy. It is very difficult in this cheery rush through a story
of childhood agony to tell exactly where Cohen thinks Pip had the
orgasm he thinks the boy is about. There's 'the trail of butter down
his leg', as Cohen puts it, which suggests he thinks Pip had it soon
after putting the bread down the trouser; and that *that* semen was the
load on the leg. But there's also, according to Cohen, the 'suspi-
ciously buttery emissions in Pip's bedroom', which suggests Pip had
his orgasm (had another?) in his bedroom and that that was what his
depositing of 'that part of my conscience' meant. But of course none
of this happened at all as Cohen interprets it. Pip is a tiny lad, too
young, I think, for orgasms even in the symbolic order. It's hard to
imagine him even as an adolescent with an erection reaching down to

103

his ankles. Cohen has never, clearly, held a slice of bread and butter. Butter doesn't 'trickle' off buttered bread, as Cohen thinks it does; buttered bread doesn't give off 'buttery emissions'. Hot buttered toast might, but this isn't hot toast. There is some buttered toast in the novel, later on, when grown-up Pip and his friends eat a lot of it at Wemmick's house – 'a haystack of buttered toast', prepared by Wemmick's Aged Parent, 'and it was delightful to see how warm and greasy we all got after it'. The Aged Parent is so greasy, says the text, that 'he might have passed for some clean old chief of a savage tribe just oiled'. And Cohen eagerly glosses all this as 'a nearly postcoital serenity at being smeared with butter from their tea and toast'. So *Great Expectations* turns into *Last Tango in Paris,* the Marlon Brando movie in which butter and coition are intimately linked! Cohen's musings do make you wonder whether he's eaten buttered toast either, but also what sex-scene he imagines as being (repressively, as he says) reproduced here. Pip and his chums in some heavy orgiastic group thing with Wemmick's old dad? But at any rate, lubricated though hot buttered toast might be, a slice of bread and butter is not, and you cannot make a slice of buttered bread into a convincing metaphor, or metonym, or symbol, or dream-figure (or whatever substitutive label you can come up with) of an ejaculating penis. Unless you're a Q Theory ideologue anxious to prove by whatever hermeneutic means, that 'at the very heart of the Victorian literary canon' there's a 'deeply saturated perversity', namely that 'One of the nineteenth-century novel's principle accomplishments is to formulate a literary language that expresses eroticism even as it designates sexuality the supremely unmentionable subject'. In other words, if wanting with Foucault to expose the Victorian text's alibis about its real interest in sexual 'perversity', you will stick at nothing, not even at clear readerly perversion of text in order to make your Theorized points.

And of course there's more, much more, bodily over-reading, not least about *Great Expectations'* great theme of touching and handling and handshakes – but I'll leave all that readerly straining about touching till later, when I praise up the virtues of readerly tact, of good or

104

better critical tactility, as the only recipe for a way out of all this Theorized mishandling.

The Eco-esque paranoia of Cohen's mishandlings owes much to the bad example of Freudian freeplay with the dream text – a freeplay continuing of course with Freud's great explicator, Jacques Lacan. Lacan is freer even than his master. And his broad-sweeping exhilaration in the presence of the linguistic, of literature, is infectious, and has infected much reading among Theorists. But what's catching is, alas, often thoroughly misleading. Lacan's poetics are truly dreadful. He really does not know how metaphor, for example, functions – as indicated all too horribly by his now famous discussion in his *Écrits* of the well-known French poem by Victor Hugo, *Booz Endormi*, about the love affair in the Bible's Book of Ruth between the old man Boaz and the young Moabitess he falls in love with as she is gleaning in his harvest fields.

The reading comes in the notorious (and highly influential) place in the *Écrits* where Lacan lays the foundations for his stock response to the Hugo poem in a strong misreading of Saussure's relationship between signifier and signified. For Saussure, these are, as I have kept on saying, always connected. Lacan drives a wedge between them, a bar, barring the passage from one to the other, expressed in his now notorious algorithm $\frac{S}{s}$, where the big Signifier (S) is shown overshadowing the meagre signified (s), which it is now, according to Lacan, quite separate from ('two distinct orders'). This algorithm, or reading, of the sign is 'not found exactly in this form in any of the numerous schemas' in the printed form of Saussure's *Cours*, but it should, says Lacan, 'be attributed' to him. (Not unlike the repressed 'truth' of masturbation in Cohen's Dickens: another presence in a text signalled by its absence.) Signification comes about, Lacan says, through relations in the top part of the algorithm, between signifiers. Metaphor occurs when one signifier substitutes for another. That's when the 'poetic spark' occurs, when 'metaphoric creation' takes place. This is a view of metaphor which would come as some surprise to regular poetics. For metaphor is surely when meaning crosses a gap between separate signs, and not simply signifiers, but when both of these signs and their meanings remain in play. There is in metaphor no absolute replacement of one sign by another, let alone an annihilation (as Lacan has it) of one term by another. That is simply not the case. The two remain connected, and their connection relies, as it began, on convincing relations (which is one reason why slice of bread and butter = penis doesn't work – except in this Lacanian view of metaphor, where any old substitution is possible).

In his illustrative reading of the Hugo poem, Lacan especially focuses on the line 'Sa gerbe n'était point avare ni haineuse': His [Booz's] sheaf was neither miserly nor spiteful. The sheaf is a metaphor, Lacan suggests, for Booz. And it annihilates him. It must do so, because sheaves of corn can't be either miserly or spiteful, whereas the man Booz can. Lacan appears, most strangely, never to have heard of the pathetic fallacy – that quintessence of metaphoric work. Clearly this false substitution theory of metaphor comes undergirded by some unawareness of the main poetic function known as prosopopoeia – personification. Booz doesn't absolutely disappear from the poem, of course; he is resurrected, as Lacan has it, in the 'abundance' that surrounds the sheaves which the desirable Ruth gets in Booz's fields, and which becomes her pregnancy and the mark of Booz's paternity.

> So, it is between the signifier in the form of the proper name of a man and the signifier that metaphorically abolishes him that the poetic spark is produced, and it is in this case all the more effective in realizing the signification of paternity in that it reproduces the mythical event in terms of which Freud reconstructed the progress, in the unconscious of all men, of the paternal mystery.

Sheaf as penis; any signifier for any signifier; no presence of signifieds: the freeplay of signifiers in a psycho-sexual reading gets sanction from the Master Freud's practice. And bad Theory – bad poetics, derived from deliberate distortion of Saussure – is the basis of a clumsy reading of a poem. The critically cannier and gratifyingly more tactful Jacques

Berthoud has said of Lacan's reading of the Hugo poem, 'What I cannot accept is a substitution theory that finds a poem and leaves it a bomb-site'. The demolition of Hugo began in Lacan's making a theoretical bomb-site out of Saussure's *Cours*.[23]

Lacan won't have us cross the bar from this dominant signifier scene to any thought of signifieds – otherwise some restraint on free substitutions, slices of bread for penises and the like, might occur. And the Theoretical bar he erects across the sign is a bar to good reading. Some version of it drops into place everywhere in Theory-constrained readings. For example, the barrier between texts and contexts set up by deconstructionists, for all Derrida's repeated protests against this, is difficult to raise, and persists in blocking the road to good reading. Even Derrida himself found it rather immovable on the important occasion when he tried publicly to clear the historicist pathway or pass in his 'Shibboleth' lecture.[24] In it he takes the Bible story (Judges 12: 4–6) of the Ephraimites trapped at a river crossing and detected as the wrong sort of people, to be killed off by Jephthah and the men of Gilead, because they can't pronounce the word *shibboleth*. This unpronounceable Hebrew word became the word in English for anything barred from speech – that which cannot be uttered, or won't be named. Derrida very cleverly takes it for what deconstructionists barred writing off from, namely context, history. He will pronounce the shibboleth of history despite his followers' aversion to it. Most cannily, he selects for a programmatically historicized reading two Paul Celan poems, 'Schibboleth' and 'In Eins', which refer to the Spanish Civil War and the republican slogan ¡*No pasarán*!, They shall not pass!: the cry of the the republican fighters barring the way to Franco's Fascists.

Herz. . . .	Driezehnter Feber. Im Herzmund
Ruf's, das Schibboleth, hinaus	erwachtes Schibboleth. Mit dir
In die Fremde der Heimat:	Peuple
Februar. No pasaran.	De Paris. *No pasarán*.
('Schibboleth', 1995)	('In Eins', 1963)

107

History is a real presence in these Celan poems, history marked by the dates they mention, apparently references to politically notable dates. These mentions configure energetically for Derrida around the 'Dreizehnter Feber', 13 February, of 'In Eins', and the 'Februar' of 'Schibboleth'. He points out that on 13 February 1963 thousands of the 'Peuple De Paris' marched in protest at a massacre by right-wing supporters of the continued French possession of Algeria. The Popular Front in France began in left-wing rioting, 12 February 1934. 'In Eins' goes on to mention the Petrograd incidents of February 1917 which led to the Russian Revolution in October of that year. Vienna fell to Fascist rightists in a February. So, says Derrida, did Madrid. 'February 1936: this [*No pasarán*] is the challenge to the fascists, to Franco's troops, to the Phalange supported by Mussolini's troops and Hitler's Condor legion: "They shall not pass" is the cry of the Republicans and the International Brigade, what they are writing on their banderoles, just before the fall of Madrid in February.' But alas for this embrace of the shibboleth of history and reference, this raising of the deconstructionist bar to history, it is calamitously wrong. The Spanish Civil War did not break out until July 1936; Madrid did not fall until early in 1939. The dates, February, 13 February, give us, Derrida asserts, 'ciphered access to this configuration'. Here, he suggests, is an indeterminacy of dating which promotes determination of meaning. In fact, he thinks, the more indeterminate the better, 'the more ample and, so to speak, populous the constelled series'. But there's some simple mistaking about Madrid and February 1936, elaborated no end by this reader, attaching to this claimed determination. In a sudden postmodernist abandonment of the dating certainties, though (perhaps there was murmuring in the audience over the Madrid mistakings: murmuring of the kind that broke out at a Spanish Civil War conference in Vienna in 1996, when a prominent French literary critic simply repeated Derrida's exposition), Derrida says he may actually be wrong about the 'so-called "external" date' of 'In Eins' – the stock deconstructionist bar to history returning at a stroke in that *so-called* and in those inverted commas. But 'even should my hypothesis be factually false, it would still designate those dates to come to which, Celan says, we write and ascribe ourselves'. The shibboleth of the contextual rearrives, then, in a rush, and dates, 'external' references, don't, apparently, matter again. Theory had returned to denigrate reference. Theory was still bad, then, for reading a poem involving dates, which became, after all, once again, simply 'dates'.

But, notably, even while those dating meanings were being briefly allowed to matter, they were going awry. Even while trying to cross the bar, the Theorist was struggling. One way or another, then, Theory proves a bar to the reading of the history-conscious text. As New Historicism, Theory's strong blend of old Marxism and newly textualized history, keeps on demonstrating.

Two examples: both from the New Historicists' recent flagship tome, *Practicing New Historicism* (2000), a veritable exhibition match of Theory, demonstrating where New Historicism has got to, how it's done, how you can Make One of These At Home, by the Theory's founder members, its CEOs, Stephen Greenblatt and Catherine Gallagher. And piss-poor it is, too, for texts, this practice of reading on *Practicing*'s model.

Stephen Greenblatt reads two sets of fifteenth-century paintings which have to do with the Christian sacrament of the eucharist: *Communion of the Apostles*, by Joost Van Ghent, and its predella (a set of painted footnotes or supplements, as it were) by Paolo Ucello. In these works, Greenblatt suggests, the question of how history and text interact is dramatized in an exemplary way, and his analysis of their interaction will be 'a model for the interpretative practice to which we aspire', i.e. New Historicism. Text, the formalist materials, the doctrinal meanings, of the paintings will not be available in any simple way by its analysis alongside the context; and nor will the historical story be simple either. There will be complex crossings and ideological concealments on either side. After all, New Historicism is about thickening up the detail in every way. And the result? At the heart of the analysis is a demonstration of textual leakage straight out of a textbook on vulgar deconstruction.

In the Joost painting Jesus extends the host, the wafer, between thumb and forefinger, to a kneeling apostle; and according to Greenblatt

109

there's nothing there, only a blank, a space: 'this blank, this dab of white in the space between the thumb and index finger of the painted Savior, is by doctrinal logic less a representation than a space where visual representation is emphatically refusing to happen'. Here, doctrine is 'at war' with the realities of an iconicity of blankness; blank signifier at odds with the alleged or desired Christian signified. Jesus says, 'Take, eat, this is my body', and that is the doctrinally sound allegation of presence, of meaning in the sign (and is traditionally taken as such). But here there's nothing, only a whiteness, no 'real presence', no transformation of bread into the body of Christ, nothing happening by any of the means the Christian church has suggested, by metaphor, by metonymy, by 'transubstantiation'. There's only absence – as certain Theory dictates – and the painting is a performance of that absence, of an *aporia*, in fact, as Greenblatt readily puts it, where the Christian doctrinal meaning of the eucharist is refusing to take place.

But this is to see in the painting only what Theory has dictated to the examining eye. Of course there's 'only' a 'dab of white' – though *dab* is a bit extreme; the ellipsis of the host looks very carefully outlined indeed. But how else, do we think, might a wafer be represented than by some white paint? This whole tussle between presence and absence, between doctrinal presence and real painted absence, has been invented by the critic, simply made up to prove a reading straight from deconstructionist stock. It's a taking of the brusquest reading, the shortest way with textual evidence: an unreading cheerfully stoked up by the parallel interpretation of the predella scene in which a miraculous bleeding host forces its way through a hole at the base of the house-door some Jewish profaners of the host (they're cooking the host) have shut against indignant Christians who want to break in and stop the blasphemy. The miraculous appearance of the blood of Christ is – in such narratives – offered by their producers as proof of the reality, the real divine presence, in the host. But, once again, Greenblatt wants the painting to deconstruct the doctrine its narrative alludes to. So the hole – a mousehole? – through which the blood escapes from the house is read and reread, variously, freely, glibly, as now wound, now bruise, now cut, or tear, or rupture. The hole can't be all of these – as the Trollopean jewel-box really can't be both vagina and testicles. And anyway it's just a hole. But *wound, tear, cut, rupture* are all lifted carefully from off the deconstructionist shelf; they're stock metaphors from the large lexicon of Derridean metaphors for afflicted writing conditions. They represent what Greenblatt wants from the painting, one more aporetic place in a text, yet another tear in the fabric of representation, one more 'site' of signifying's 'resistance and disruption', yet another wounded, marred text, one more fraught emblem of 'the representational dilemma'.[25]

There is much of interest in Greenblatt's analysis; even some of his generalizations are arresting ones. 'Aporias are not places where forms refer only to themselves, but are rather the tears where energies, desires, and repression flow out into the world.' What a nice idea. The trouble is that this is the gloss on two painted scenes in which there isn't any *aporia*, either in the real whiteness of the Joost 'dab' of paint, or in the 'wound-bruise-cut-tear-rupture' of the Ucello mousehole. The reading of the signifying 'holes' is just full of holes.

Which is also the case with Catherine Gallagher's analysis in *Practicing New Historicism* of nineteenth-century representations of Irishness as a problem emblematized in hostile Protestant perceptions of what the Catholic Irish fed off – namely the Body of Christ, the sacramental wafer, and the potato. It's a canny pairing and a devastating allegation. The 'most horrific anti-potato rhetoric seems to borrow the extreme literalism of eucharistic doctrine when it turns to the relation between body and food'. And William Cobbett's letters from Ireland are offered as the great example of this rhetoric. In them, according to Gallagher, the Irish are shown living underground, 'like their food, literally in the soil'; 'in low mud huts, full of holes'. Cobbett's 'subterranean imagery' reduces the Irish labourers 'to something quite a bit lower than pigs – something closely resembling pigs'. But when you go and look at Cobbett's (admittedly) awed Letter No. 3 from Kilkenny in the *Political Register* (11 October 1834), which Gallagher is allegedly glossing and quoting, you find she is in fact seriously misquoting and highly misleading. Cobbett is by no means simply

111

anti–potato, but in favour of meat and bread as better modes of sustenance (and was he not proved correct by the 1840s potato famine?). The Irish people's huts are not mud; but 'rough stone and mud whited over'; they're not especially low, either, being about nine feet high; they are not all without 'any windows at all', as Gallagher alleges, for some have 'a glass window'. Nor is it Cobbett who is reducing the Irish to an animal–like existence, life in 'a hole', with animals for companions and pig–like food to eat: he's charging the English landlords with doing that.[26]

Materialist imagination? Material misleadings of the imagination, rather. E. P. Thompson's word for 'what if' historiography comes to mind: *Geschichtenscheissenschlopff* – history as shitty–slop.[27] Once again the New Historicist fails to read what's there in a text, driven by Theory's limited idea of signification and especially by her Theorized disposition to import aporetic multi–gappiness into her chosen emblems of Irishness, the eucharistic host and the potato, her Irish analogue of the eucharist. The 'potato did not restrict itself to one meaning; it was as ambivalent, arbitrary, historically overdetermined, unstable, and opaque as any other signifier'. If you come believing that Irish signification, like all signification, is all holes (to the point of opacity: as one keeps seeing, textual metaphors do have a way of freely combining in Theory's discourses!), so that what signifies Irishness – the host and the potato, and the host-eater and the potato-eater – must also be full of holes, then of course you're likely to find them. Especially if you're unscrupulous in your reading. And Theoretical predisposition is indeed promoting here an unscrupulosity of reading which is apparently most successful in finding what is sought – no matter that the proof-texts on offer suggest differently.

Again and again you find Theory working like this. Theory blurs texts. It has people misreading; reading otherwise in a bad sense; reading against the textual grain; against the verbal, the literary, odds; against good sense; against some very plain senses of the words. Theory just tears up the literature, the letters, whose readings it sponsors; and it does so with the ample resources in the thick stock of the Theory gumbo. When a Theorist goes to town, he really goes to town, spooning up the stock responses thick and threefold, and all to the same damaging effect. As when J. Hillis Miller attends to Thomas Hardy's poem 'The Torn Letter':

I

I tore your letter into strips
No bigger than the airy feathers
That ducks preen out in changing weathers
Upon the shifting ripple-tips.

II

In darkness on my bed alone
I seemed to see you in a vision,
And hear you say: 'Why this derision
Of one drawn to you, though unknown?'

III

Yes, eve's quick need had run its course,
The night had cooled my hasty madness;   10
I suffered a regretful sadness
Which deepened into real remorse.

IV

I thought what pensive patient days
A soul must know of grain so tender,
How much of good must grace the sender
Of such sweet words in such bright phrase.

V

Uprising then, as things unpriced
I sought each fragment, patched and mended;
The midnight whitened ere I had ended
And gathered words I had sacrificed.   20

VI

But some, alas, of those I threw
Were past my search, destroyed for ever:
They were your name and place; and never
Did I regain those clues to you.

VII

I learnt I had missed, by rash unheed,
My track; that, so the Will decided,
In life, death, we should be divided,
And at the sense I ached indeed.

VIII

That ache for you, born long ago,
Throbs on: I never could outgrow it.   30
What a revenge, did you but know it!
But that, thank God, you do not know.[28]

It's a poem full of mysteries and withheld information. What's the
gender of the letter's sender? What's the real relationship between the
letter-writer and the letter's addressee? Why the tearing up, the guilt?
In what sense was the sender of the letter 'unknown' (line 8). When
was 'long ago'? Was the 'ache for you, born long ago' (29) the ache
caused by tearing up the letter, or some earlier ache? If it was the
latter, how is that qualified by the 'unknown' of line 8? Hillis Miller is
not terribly interested in these questions patently raised by any literal-
ist reading. He quickly opts for assuming the sender is female. He
doesn't notice the allusion to the Bible's David and Jonathan story ('in
their death they were not divided') in lines 26–7 – 'so the Will [the
Schopenhauerean Will which decides fates in Hardy's fiction] decided,
In life, death, we should be divided' – which might have a bearing on
the gender question. What Miller goes for, and typically of Theorists'
readings, is allegory: the poem as an allegory of how letters, epistles,
and thus the whole art of writing and the business of reading, proceed. Which might be all right – it's perfectly possible to raise read-

114

ings up to the allegorical level, provided you get the literal level sorted out first. The trouble is that Miller comes to his allegorical interpretation his belly stuffed full of Theory gumbo, bearing allegedly parallel texts he has also been reading along Theoretical lines, and quite bowed down by the weight of Derrida's influential discussions of how letters and postcards work (in *La Carte Postale*, 1980), and particularly their relation to telepathy – letters are telepathic, long-distance communications, which can produce their recipients (Derrida, 'Télépathie', in *Furor*, 1981). And the result is a kind of glorious non-reading, a set of more or less irrelevancies. Miller really can't see the poetic wood for the Theory trees he's planted in the way.

The main parallel text he adduces is a letter from Kafka to his girl-friend Milena on the subject of letter-writing – about how letters are non-communicative because 'ghosts', the ghosts of the recipient and of the writer, drink up the writing, the 'written kisses', on their journey. This Kafka passage, highly appealing to the Theorist who wants to stress the purely phantom nature of the writer and the recipient (something Kafka never suggests: he never thought of himself as a mere phantom, nor of Milena as purely phantasmic: they were both of them all too painfully real to each other for such a thought), is to be applied, really quite gratuitously, to the Hardy. (Miller also, by the way, misses out from his quotation from Kafka, Kafka's words about human beings not liking this ghostly separation of letter-writers, and inventing the train, the car and the aeroplane to fight it, and then Kafka's wondering whether the telegraph, the telephone and 'radio-telegraphy' are any improvement on letters.) Kafka's ghostly recipient is then hooked onto Derrida's paradoxical definition of the reader of telepathic letters – 'one cannot say of the recipient that he exists before the letter'. And that's layered onto the poem – both Hardy's 'I' and his 'You' becoming for Miller absolutely ghostly. But this is to ignore the fact that he/she wasn't always dead, and if (s)he's a ghost now (s)he wasn't always one. And his/her letter came from someone living, and although it was torn up and defaced, the name and address thus getting lost, there was indeed a name and address attached to it once. But Miller, enamoured of Paul de Man's tendentious suggestion that apostrophe (addressing someone) is always a talking with the dead, and that prosopopoeia, personification, is really a rhetoric of death and absence, a defacement/depersonification, brings that in to colour up the negativity of the allegory he's drawing. Furthermore Saussure's hypograms, those ghostly nominal presences Saussure thought he might detect as acrostics in texts, are mentioned to illustrate how the ghostly presences of the sender and recipient might be brought into existence in the poem. 'Again, as in Saussure's hypograms, what is "proper" to the letter is not a proper name and place attached to it on the outside but a power distributed throughout its minutest parts, its letters, a power to bring into existence the phantom selves of both sender and destined receiver.' Never mind that Saussure wisely abandoned the hypogrammatic quest as a bad job and a blind alley: nothing will stop Miller drawing on Theory's inflated reserves. The torn letter becomes an emblem of textual multivalence. 'The letter by no means has the "organic unity" that used to be attributed to the single text. It can be turned into a thousand tiny pieces.' A jeer that, at Theory's *bête noire* of 'organic unity', which will be got in – despite that despised 'unity' being of a thematic, conceptual kind, not to be confused with the mere materiality of the paper the text is written on. And where did those 'thousand tiny pieces' come from? They're not in the poem. And going allegorical with the letter's fragments Miller has no time, naturally, to reflect on the poem's most arresting image and locution: the 'shifting ripple-tips' of the water the ducks of stanza 1 shed their 'airy feathers' onto. Dipping into Theory's gumbo-bowl is more important, it would appear, than listening to the poem's extraordinary local way with words.

And so it goes. The poem's allusion to missing 'My track' is blurred up with yet another stock Theory-world reference, this time to Borges's story *The Garden of Forking Paths* ('It is as if he were two separate persons, or two superposed persons, the one who took the track and the one who did not take it, as in Borges's . . .'). *As if.* That's really pushing the poem about. (*As if* and *as though* work very hard in Miller's reading: they have to.) The Borges allusion is (of course) backed up by a bit of Nietzsche on the divisibility of the self – interesting in itself, but only relevant on the back of the irrelevant Borges. And really riffing, improvising like crazy in fact, on Derrida ('there is no' person/self/recipient before he/she 'receives the letter', which is not precisely what Derrida said), Miller ends up suggesting that 'The reader of "The Torn Letter" becomes not so much, through a familiar kind of negative capability, the self of the speaker-writer of the poem, the "I" who has received the letter and is haunted by it, as, by a far stranger form of metamorphosis, the "you" to whom the poem is spoken or written. The reader becomes the woman who has caused the "I" so much ache'. Really? The association of the reader's self with the "I" of poem surely only happens when that *I* does or feels something the reader can actually associate with (falling in love, feeling melancholy, and so on); it's most unlikely that many readers would put or find themselves in the very specific short-story-like circumstances of this poem's tearer-up of the letter. And why, anyway, would that process be a negative capability – surely a case of severe abuse of Keats's famous 'negative capability'? And by what strange metamorphosis would the *you* become *me*, the poem's recipient? 'You, hypocrite lecteur, mon semblable, mon frère': that, from Eliot's *The Waste Land*, touches me in a way. 'Let us go then, you and I': Prufrock's invitation touches me far less. I only feel addressed by a poem's *you* when it's appropriate and apt; and I certainly don't feel any personal contact with the person who wrote or writes to Thomas Hardy's 'I'. And that person is, to repeat, not certainly a woman. And making me, the reader, a woman, is only a bit of Feminist-inspired wishful thinking, some fashionable gender-bending to keep the Derrideanism company.

The whole reading is a farrago of Theory bluff; it's all Theory guff. Not the least fanciful bit of which cheery perversity is where the critic rhapsodizes about the alleged telepathic contact between Hardy and Derrida:

> Hardy's poem, which is a 'letter' in the first person written to an unnamed 'you', has found its proper recipient at last in the unwitting Derrida. Derrida has become its reader without ever knowing it. He has been programmed by the poem to write an

interpretation of it, before, beside, or after the letter, so to speak, in displacement from any conscious encounter with it. He has become the person the poem–letter invites him to be, in a confirmation of his theories of which he is unaware.

Which is, of course, rubbish. Theory-driven, though. And misreading, like all Miller's reading of this poem (Derrida never suggested a letter would make its own recipient if (s)he never read it). It's the most laughable bit of stock responding within this wholesale headlong plunge of Miller's along Theory's supermarket shelves, optimistically filling his trolley with keys to the poem, most of which simply don't unlock a thing in it.[29]

Stock responses trigger misreading, they set readers chasing off happily in directions of Theory's choosing, rather than those of the text in front of them. And there's always that escalating tendency which Miller illustrates so nicely: with a single Theory-empowered bound or two, the reader and the reading fly straight up and beyond the words in the particular text, out to the vastest generalizing spaces of Theory's philosophical universe. And it's usually some very tendentious grand generalization – like Miller's many – that is produced from the reading hat and waved at the audience; much of it just linguistic and philosophical non-sense. But then, Theory's claims are large – and Grand Theory is unafraid of even the largest generalization – so the scope for large nonsenses is indeed huge. And Theorists rarely fail us here.

Take the conclusions typically drawn by readers of Beckett – conclusions which scarcely square with what the particular texts of Beckett's anguish suggest, but ones which fit rather the stock conclusions of the Theory Beckett's work is being sieved through. 'Just as there is no longer a difference between, say, poetry and prose, there is no longer a difference between the real and its opposite. Could it be fiction, as Borges understands it? All is fiction. Language is all that remains.' Theory's brush sweeps away everything but language, in the name of Beckett (and Borges), and with a briskness neither writer would begin to comprehend. The 'text has conclusively demonstrated, like most of the late Beckett texts, that seeing is imagining'. No, claiming that what is, in reality, there to be seen is actually only produced by the imagination of the observer (or 'observer') is what Theory has concluded, not Beckett. 'Memory, as every reader of *Molloy* knows, is only another name for invention.' No, that's not what reading *Molloy* will tell you ('Wrong, very rightly wrong' is *Molloy*'s corrective to the thought that 'Saying is inventing').

> By everywhere undermining the connection between language and reality, Beckett has deliberately run words aground, leaving them no longer usable as signs for meanings beyond themselves, but oddly free to express meaning by reference to other words. . . . Once the referential function of language has been exposed as a sham, the lyrical is put on an equal footing with the less than lyrical. . . . The language of Beckett's minimalist fiction can, by definition, cut away everything but language. And once language is accepted as relying not on external 'reality' for its significance but is understood rather as the source of its own meaning, the more poetic, more conventional use of it lends at least a linguistic significance.

Which is singing from Theory's hymn-sheet with a vengeance, a Rhapsody in Theory, a running of Theory's non-referentialist/differentialist yardstick over Beckett's texts with only travesty as a result – travesty deep and wide, travesty insulting to the author and his writing, and to all undogmatized readers. Nothing in Beckett's texts, late or early, separates language from reality, or supposes language is the sole source of its own meaning, or leaves you with nothing but language. The body and mind in pain, the self troubled by theology and morality and history and bad legs and withering physique and death are what drive Beckett's texts from start to finish of his career. The question of how the imagination copes with these manifold distresses of the physical and spiritual real, of how words rise (and fall and rise again) to the occasions of the rendering of these infirmities, is a question, even *the* question: 'the proportion of invention vast

assuredly vast proportion a thing you don't know the threat the bleeding arse the cracking nerves you invent but real or imaginary no
knowing it's impossible it's not said it doesn't matter it does it did
that's superb a thing that matters'. That's *How It Is*, and how it is in
Beckett's texts. His writings contemplate 'the bleeding arse the cracking
nerves' as awesome realities, the things that matter, apprehended at
the place where the real and the imaginary dauntingly converge.[30]
Only vulgar Theory would simplify the complexity of that place of
signification. Only the conceptual and hermeneutical vulgarity of
Theorists; only Theory's Stock Responses. About which, hear again
the wisdom of I. A. Richards:

> A stock response, like a stock line in shoes or hats, may be a
> convenience. Being ready-made, it is available with less trouble
> than if it had to be specially made out of raw or partially pre-
> pared materials. . . . Indeed, an extensive repertory of stock re-
> sponses is a necessity. Few minds could prosper if they had to
> work out an original, 'made to measure' response to meet every
> situation that arose – their supplies of mental energy would be
> too soon exhausted and the wear and tear on their nervous sys-
> tems would be too great. Clearly there is an enormous field of
> conventional activity over which acquired, stereotyped, habitual
> responses properly rule, and the only question that needs to be
> examined as to *these* responses is whether they are the best that
> practical exigencies – the range of probable situations that may
> arise, the necessity of quick availability and so forth – will allow.
> But equally clearly there are in most lives fields of activity in
> which stock responses, if they intervene, are disadvantageous and
> even dangerous, because they may get in the way of, and pre-
> vent, a response more appropriate to the situation. These un-
> necessary misfits may be remarked at almost every stage of the
> reading of poetry . . .

They are certainly 'to be remarked at almost every stage of the reading' of literature compelled by Theory. And to use Richards's mild

terms of disapproval, they are disadvantageous, dangerous even, because they do indeed 'get in the way of a response more appropriate
to the situation'. They lack the tact I shall advocate as the key to more
appropriate responding.

8

Theory Shrinks

> Accustomed as we are to strip a whole page of its sentences and crush their meaning out in one grasp, the obstinate resistance which a page of *Urne Burial* offers at first trips us and blinds us.
> Virginia Woolf, 'Reading'

Theory's claim is to open all literary doors. Like George Eliot's Revd Mr Casaubon in *Middlemarch*, Theory wants to provide the Key – or keys – to All Mythologies, to all literary mythologies. It would be the biggest troper around. Its aim is to enable the reading of all possible texts. The hermeneutic grip Theory desires to offer texts could not be larger. All literary Theory comes out of, it *is*, Grand Theory. But in practice this large reach, this vast grasp, this expansive vision, is a route to diminishment. Literary Theory in fact diminishes the literary, diminishes texts, by reducing them to formulae, to the formulaic, to the status only of the model, of models of literary functions, even of the literary at large, but still only a model. The latest text to be analysed turns out to be only another illustration of this or that Theoretical position or line. There is a slot for this one, a box that fits, already made. The critical results, the outcomes of reading, thus keep on being the same, or very similar. Difference is annihilated in this modelling rush; it's unwelcome; it is ignored. All the texts of, say, Beckett, get hoovered up into the same bag, and it's the bag the Theorizing critic brought along with her. One size, one model, fits all. Mess, contingency, overflow, surplus, somebody doing something a bit different with the old forms, being different from the next author, the next text, the text before this one in an *oeuvre*, any resistance to being reduced or limited to some given model – all the singularities and variations that ordinary readers actually look for in the next novel (say) they take off the bookshop shelf, or home from the library, or download from the internet, and settle down to read (even though this quest for difference is often a disappointing one) – are not what Theorized reading is seeking, unless, of course, it can Theorize these surpluses and extras and thus grant them Theoretical sameness too.

This is a Theoretical reduction commonly complained of. A. S. Byatt, for example, shrewd critic as well as a novelist thoroughly alert to Theory, has the hero-narrator of her novel *The Biographer's Tale* (2000) resign from being a poststructuralist teacher of literature in order to go in instead for biography:

> One of the reasons I had given up poststructuralist thought was the disagreeable amount of imposing that went on in it. You decided what you were looking for, and then duly found it – male hegemony, liberal-humanist idées reçues, etc. This was made worse by the fact that deconstructionists and others paid lip-service to the idea that they must not impose – they even went so far as half-believing they must not find either. And yet they discovered the same structures, the same velleities, the same evasions quite routinely in the most disparate texts. I wanted most seriously *not* to impose that sort of reading.

Of course, this critic-turned-biographer soon discovers that biography is not all plain-sailing, and that there are velleities and evasions at every turn in the textual materials he takes to working with, and even certain conclusions to be drawn from his investigations of a sort of deconstructionist kind. But his suspicions and resistances are well-founded. Theory goes in for more of the same, and such describing inevitably involves a reduction of writing to just one, or a mere few, features. Here's yet another case of the aporetic, or whatever: a stunning one, maybe, but still just one more. Theory monodicizes, monodicizes texts, monodicizes readers. Theory invites you to read as a woman, a Marxist, a Deconstructionist, a Neo-Historicist, a Postcolonialist, or a Derridean or Lacanian or Foucauldian, as some such Theory singleton – as once you were invited to profess yourself a New Critic or a Leavisite, or for that matter an editor of texts, a biographer, a philologist, a literary historian. Theory invites you to profess a single kind of interest in a writing, to shut out, if only *pro tempore*, other readings, other reading selves than just the one. Which is truly ironic in a critical era commanded by noisy urgings to respect the multivalence of texts and to resist the univalent, monodic interpretative outcome as an outmoded simplicity.

This reductiveness is not, as I've suggested, absolutely new. Ideologies have always thinned analysis, blinkered analysts, made complex objects dreadfully simple. Here comes, you might think, another complex rag-bag of tissue and emotions, but no, the Calvinist sees only a sinner predestined to hell; the Marxist sees only a bourgeois rentier; the free-marketeer recognizes a mere shopper. And for simple ease of making one's way around the complexity of phenomena, such shorthand – the stock response, in fact – comes in handy. As I. A. Richards recognized. But shorthand is shorthand, an approach involving much loss, especially when you're dealing with persons and person-products – of which literature is a very strong, perhaps the strongest, case. T. S. Eliot's J. Alfred Prufrock knows how confining is the formulating gaze, 'The eyes that fix you in a formulated phrase'. 'And when I am formulated, sprawling on a pin / When I am pinned and wriggling on the wall', then the space for ordinary bodily and social and verbal functions is utterly stymied.

> Then how should I begin
> To spit out all the butt-ends of my days and ways?
> And how should I presume?

Literary theory has often gone in for Calvinist- or Marxist-style reducings, for systematic theology in fact. Many theorists have been Calvinists and Marxists and systematic theologians, as well as secularized versions of such. It's no accident that Terry Eagleton the Marxist was

124

once Terry Eagleton the Roman Catholic. The influential system-building of Northrop Frye, his deftly interlocking critical anatomies, come, quite clearly, out of the systematizing dispositions of his Calvinist, or post-Calvinistic Christianity. But Frye's devoted modellings – here comes another case of the motif of winter, or of menippean satire, or some other literary instance from his craftily dovetailed suite of critical cupboards – are only very clear cases of Theory's regular tendency to define, that is to read, by the pigeon-holing label.[1]

Literary theorizing has always worked by the label, the sticker, the tag – biographical fallacy, intentionalism, sentimentalism, realism, and so on. And we like these – after all, they do so much of our interpretation for us. We like them so much, we plunder them from all over – from rhetoric, from genre, from prosody, from linguistics. But whatever their particular pedigree they're used as quick hermeneutic devices and markers. This is a catachretical text, or a sonnet/epic/satire/tragedy, an iambic pentameter, or a hysteron proteron, we say, seeking to convey meaning, to do reading, to further the critical conversation. And indeed we are being hermeneutical, conveying meaning, doing reading, up to a point. To be sure, there's always a certain laziness here; this can be reading as it were by numbers, by algorithm, a kind of automated, mechanistic hermeneutics. A reader like the pioneering Theorist Vladimir Propp, for example, is very clear that this is exactly what he wants: to systematize the reading business, to make classifying Russian folktales as certain a matter as Linnaeus's botanical classification, to cut out interpretative uncertainty, the mess of individual judgement, to put some scientific rigour into *Literaturwissenschaft*, into literary-science. Which is, of course, to cut down the amount of attention – of engagement – required of the individual reader. And this is Theory's point. Propp's *Morphology of the Folktale* is not only a foundational structuralist work, it is a model of Theory's practices and aspirations, and particularly in this – that a great goal of Theory is to make reading simple. Theory's shorthand, its signposting of literary routes, its labellings, are there to ease interpretative labour. Propp is quite open about how his classifications of folktale functions should make the interpreter's life easier. They're an interpreter's yardstick which you only have to run over the material to define it precisely. 'Just as cloth can be measured with a yardstick to determine its length, tales may be measured by the scheme and thereby defined.'[2] If you are this way minded the provision of yardsticks is the very beauty of Theory.

Even if we do not call ourselves Theorists, we all do have our critical yardsticks. They're in the critical tool-kit we bring to every reading job. We all of us rely to a large extent on such markers. And texts do indeed have common and recurrent features which the conventional yardsticks we bring are useful for accessing. Our yardsticks are our canons of interpretation, of course: *canon* – rod, stick, yardstick, ruler, rule. And we need them: our canon-rulers are not only most useful in making headway with a text, to making sense, they're clearly essential. But however revelatory, they are clearly only good for the opening shots at reading. Reading must go further than our shorthand tags will take us. By definition they stop short. They don't go the whole hog, don't utter the whole thing. Shorthand is short. And the problem with Theory is that it encourages, as never before, this shortening of attention, this not going far enough, this reading laziness in fact. And one trouble is that the alleged power of Theory's tags, the vividness and breadth and range of their critical claims (this is Grand Theory, remember), as well as their attractive novelty (at first, at least), seduces us into the illusion that much more of serious readerly meaning is being obtained by their use (far surpassing, it's claimed, the limitations and amateurishness of earlier critical times), than is actually the case. The flash and crash and thunder of Theory's labelling blinds and deafens us, in other words, to its real littleness, the belittling work of all theory, but of our Theory especially.

How they abound, and how fertile they seem and have seemed, these allegories of reading in a word or phrase, the whole critical world apparently in a jug, stories of reading in a nutshell. They're so snappy, handily snappy, hermeneutical snaps, snapshots, cosmoses of critical meaning and force in a memorable word, a phrase. Many of them French, too, reflecting the authority of the exotic critical Other out there, the passing excitements of Theory's word from Paris:

126

Il n'y a pas de hors texte. Mise en abyme. Différence. Différance. Difference not reference. Béance. Jeu. Play. Freeplay. Jeu des signifiants. Sign. Signifier. Signified. Binary opposition. Floating signifier. Transcendental signified. Synchrony. Diachrony. Langue. Parole. Sous râture. Écriture. Écriture feminine. Scriptible. Coupure. Break. Gap. Lack. Rupture. *Aporia.* Two interpretations of interpreting. Significance. Signification. Signifying. The Death of the Author. Presence. Absence. Logocentric. Phallocentric. Theologocentric. Phallogocentric. Patriarchalism. Multivalence. Dialogism. Carnivalesque. Dream work. The return of the repressed. Performative utterance. The anxiety of influence. Gaze. Power. Structured like a language. Unheimlich. Body. $\frac{S}{s}$.

Paid-up admirers of Derrida used to deny that deconstruction could be reduced to a handy lexicon or list of this (or the NAS) kind. But Derrida himself wields the list as an informative tool or map of his business. 'For me', he writes to his Japanese Friend, deconstruction 'lets itself be determined by such other words as "écriture", "trace", "différance", "supplement", "hymen", "pharmakon", "marge", "entame", "parergon", etc.' This 'naming is done only for reasons of economy', Derrida adds.[3] But that's exactly the reason for such naming. (The Sokal hoax would not have come off had Sokal's piece not been liberally larded with such names and namings, the lullingly reassuring, thought-saving buzzwords and bullet-points from the Theory handbook, the shibboleths of Theory business.) And of course these names, this instant terminology of Theory, do convey meaning. They mark critical territory, indicate critical positions, invite and evoke particulars of reading. If they were not real and functional critical markers that NAS hit-list I quoted earlier would lack any force as either description or warning.

But this is a way of cutting texts down to size, to the limited size of whatever interpretative dimension the label seeks to encapsulate. For Theory means reduction. It involves inevitable reduction. It has to, as soon as it offers, as it does, access by hermeneutical formulae, algorithms, models, maps. Vladimir Propp, the frankest of Theorists, is clear that this reductiveness is Theory's goal. 'Knowing how moves are distributed, we can decompose every tale into its components.' Like the good Theorist he is, he has his codification system all poised for encountering every next story to come along. Thirty-one functions of dramatis personae, all labelled with letters and arrows, with subdivisions of function indicated by superscript numbers, make up the map or algorithmic model of all Russian folktales, indeed, allegedly, of all folktales anywhere. Thirty-one functions. The great reductiveness of this analytical embrace of the huge phenomenon of folktale, the large phenomenological field this fiction comprises, is clear. Every arriving example will fit, or be made to fit, into the Theory's scheme. Every particular case is reduced to a mere instance of the formulae. So that analysis (which is reading, interpretation, remember) of, say, 'The Swan-Geese' story comes out as

$$\gamma^1\beta^1\delta^1A^1C\uparrow\left\{\begin{array}{c}[DE^1 \text{ neg. } F \text{ neg.}]\\ d^7E^7F^9\end{array}\right\}G^4K^1\downarrow[Pr^1D^1E^1F^9 = Rs^4]^3 \qquad [4]$$

A computer could reckon like this. Truths about 'The Swan-Geese' are being conveyed. This is reading of a sort. But it is reductive. The result is a truly dinkified version of 'The Swan-Geese', based on a reductive theoretical formulation of the ways of the whole fictional genre or category the story has been put in. And all Theoretical readings are, in essence, like this. Every time a reading 'comes out' (Henry James again), much like Propp's, as another case of *aporia* or phallogocentrism or the (free)play of the signifier, or whatever it might be from the Theory catalogue, dinkification is what is happening. And dinkifying is, indeed, catachretical, distortion by limitation, by reduction. As knowledge goes, this is knowing by knowing *less*. This is getting a hermeneutic hold on textual reality whose interpretative power is dependent on a kind of asset-stripping.

And this is inevitable. It is of the very nature of the model, the map, which it is Theory's business to provide the reader with. Maps have to be dinky versions of the real they seek to describe. They are pocket battleships, as it might be, with a certain real fire-power, but still they're for the pocket. This is the nature of the formula, the model, the map. To be at all useful a map has to go in your pocket, it must be able to be held in the hand, must be portable. 'Let him [the traveller] carry with him also some card [i.e. map] or book describing the country where he travelleth, which will be a good key to his inquiry.' Thus Francis Bacon in his essay 'Of Travel' (1635). The map, the guide-book, can be useful keys, but only if they're book-sized, on a card. Maps relate to phenomena handily, but only handily. Like mobile phones – known in German as *Handys* – they're only useful if they can be held in the hand. They model phenomena usefully, but only because they reduce the phenomenally real, when they scale things down. And in this they're a nice allegory, or model, of the sense-making effort, the reading-effort, as it affects both writers and readers, but especially of the work of Theory. Maps tell us a lot, like the theorizing effort they model. Theorizing is a kind of cartography, but with all a map's pitfalls, not least its essential belittling work.

Making any progress at all around the surface of the earth demands a map. We know our way about our home-place, our neighbour-hood, only because we have internalized a map of it. The first thing anyone venturing into *terra incognita* tries to do is to make a map of it. Being equipped with a map is essential to finding your way around the strange place, different terrain, the foreign city. Without a map the city is a maze you can't read, a kind of signifying blank, certainly a puzzle. Roland Barthes vividly explains the problem in his *Empire of Signs*. He simply can't get around central Tokyo without a guide to it, and he can't obtain any published guide. To make his sexual rendez-vous he needs the sketch maps his contacts supply him with. And for us to follow him, we his readers need the maps he now supplies to us in his book.[5] The published map is the first step to making the public place one's private possession. And reading, making sense, is always like this; it needs a map.

One of the most striking things about the traditional detective story, the archetypical fiction of getting around, of finding the way about the place, a set of fictions which is openly about cracking open the secrets and confusions of the moral maze, is how the genre goes in for the map. Knowing and showing where things and people are, and where the cadavers were, is of the genre's essence, and providing literal maps to assist that knowing is, clearly, essential to that need of the genre. Maps are central to the detective novel's epistemology and hermeneutic. Drawing them was probably very useful in the first place to the writer. Writers, especially novelists, often need maps to help keep their plots straight – Stephen King's wall-charts, Trollope's maps of his Barsetshire,[6] Dickens's chapter plans and notes to himself ('No Steerforth this time. Keep him out. Then on to Em'ly. Divide last chapter in two', and so on).[7] Revealingly, the great Vladimir Nabokov thought that reading only made any headway at all by mapping, in one form or another. His lectures at Wellesley and Cornell in the 1940s relied utterly on his own private mappings. He listed the structural features of *Bleak House* (nine of them: a breakdown resembling, as it were, Barthes's five narrative codes in his *S/Z*, or, in little, Propp's great effort in reducing the Russian folktale to thirty-one functions). He annotated the published lists of characters to be found at the front of his copy of *Bleak House* ('Good', 'Evil', 'Very Good', 'Mild', and so on: a privatizing of the published map – and, in ways not unexpected from the author of *Lolita*, the four Dickens girls he shortlists are 'all flushing prettily. All belong to one genus little nymphs attending to wants of other people'). He made himself a 'chart of the main themes' in *Bleak House*, the 'Chancery theme', the 'Child theme' and the 'Mystery theme'; it was a map of intersecting and interacting people and topics – his 'Formula', as he put it, 'of the Book in form of themes'. And he charted all the main locations of the novel on a sketch map of England. These mappings were first of all for his own understanding, and then for his students' benefit. 'Open your books at the list of characters', is the instruction this lecturer has scribbled on his 'Chart of main themes'. He'll have his students begin their reading where he began his, with his annotation of the map of characters in the copy of the novel he shares with them. Such charts, such formulaic abstractions were, in Nabokov's kept-up view, the only access to such large fictions as *Bleak House*. To understand *Ulysses*, you needed, he said, a street map of Dublin; to get on with *Anna Karenina* a plan of the compartments on the Moscow–Petersburg railway trains was essential; he drew plans of Gregor Samsa's apartment to illustrate Kafka's *Metamorphosis*; and so forth. And who would quarrel with this stress on mapping?[8] Mapping is, in effect, what reading requires. We all, in our private way, do, more or less, what Nabokov did, as steps into fictions. And Theory is nothing less than the making public, the granting of wide valency to this activity. So if some form of theory is always a prerequisite of understanding, it is essentially the directional help of the map that is being sought from theory. And of course it is no accident that theoretical works keep indulging in the chart, the map, not only metaphorically, but actually. Theory's abstractions are, often, like Propp's formulae, quite literally a mapping. As is, say, A. J. Greimas's commonly reproduced scheme of *actants*, those general categories of action which he alleged to underlie all the doings of characters in fiction (the *acteurs*): essentially a map of how Greimas's six actants relate (six actants summarizing all acteurs, as Propp's thirty-one functions of character are proposed as encapsulating all possible personae in the folktale):

Sender → Object → Receiver
      ↑
Helper → Subject ← Opponent

All of fictional transactions in a single simple narratological diagram, map, model (based, of course, on Jakobson's basic communication model). And how it, and variants of it, packed analyses of fiction in the High Theory period of the 1970s and 1980s. And the map has its revelatory uses, as, in their way, do Dickens's chapter plans, Nabokov's maps for *Bleak House*, and those scribbled guides to Barthes's Tokyo assignations. But the point that has to be stressed is that, as with all maps, or models, or formulae, this usefulness is contingent, absolutely contingent, upon a great deal being left out of the account that the model/map renders. And this is an overlooked muchness which in the circumstances, the circumstances of reading, whether of a novel or a city, really does need to be accounted for if what is sought is fuller knowledge, fuller acquaintance, than any mapping, however full or fulsome it be, can in the end provide. And, presumably, it is precisely such fuller knowledge which in the end the reader really wants. To truly experience Tokyo you do have to do more than just look at the map of it; you have to essay those marked streets for yourself; really get your hands on the places (and people) the map only sketchily implies. And so it is with reading. Theory's maps may help, but its maps, like any map, will always need supplementing, supplementing by the reading equivalent of walking down the street for yourself, opening doors, getting inside, having the hands-on contacts and experiences Barthes's navigations led him to.

For whatever conceptual grasp the map manages, whatever its descriptive force and analytic power, its power in organizing access to a text or group of textual phenomena, these are purchased at the expense of distinct disadvantages. Theory's wrenching, distortive way with the text, that suspicion of texts I talked of earlier in this argument, reaches here a kind of malignant apotheosis in the necessary shrinkage which all maps must effect. Making small is what Milton's God did to the rebellious angels in *Paradise Lost* Book II: he shrank them and then he shrank their city, Pandaemonium. Being made small is God's judgement on devils; it's God's marker of devilishness. Becoming cramped, losing elbow room – in 'narrow room', the now midget streets of their city, the devils 'throng numberless' – is the discontent of the overpowered, a judgement on the desire to stretch out, to take over God's large place, to make for themselves more *Lebensraum* illegitimately. Theorists and Theory, in shrinking texts, as they do, are acting cruelly on texts; the judgement involved is punitive.

On the other hand, shrinkage is a kind of idolatry, on the Judaeo-Christian model, biblical idolatry. This idolatry is worshipping false gods, having other gods before God, and doing so by shrinking the divine, reducing the large, difficult, messy real presence of Jehovah to the small knowable fetish object, the golden calf in the wilderness. In his truly insightful 1995 Ernest Jones lecture to the British Psychoanalytical Society, the poet and Oxford Professor of Poetry James Fenton asked of Sigmund Freud and his giant horde of tiny effigies and doll-like figurines, which Freud took everywhere with him obsessively, transplanting them carefully from his home in Vienna to his exile in London: did Freud worship idols, making unto himself, as it were, graven images in disobedience to the Ten Commandments? Fenton leaves the question dangling.[9] But, of course, in serious ways, Freud did worship idols – as a theorist, an arch-theorist, one of the great arche-theorists of our Theory movement, he modelled the human self, formulating it in terms of his small, but extraordinarily potent set of person-components – consciousness, subconsciousness, ego, id, libido, superego, oedipus complex – the highly reductive small group (far fewer than Propp's thirty-one functions, not many more than Barthes's five codes) of functional areas of the human. Of course Freud worshipped idols. All Theorists do. Theory makes idols, eidolons, dolls, toys, out of texts, out of literature. And the whole deity, the whole person, the whole text thus reduced cries out to be allowed to expand, to grow up, to have its whole self back again. It's a cry figured by Jane Eyre when she's taken by Mr Rochester to a silk warehouse to be kitted out and fitted up in expensive clothing, like a puppet woman, and resists. 'I can never bear being dressed like a doll by Mr Rochester': she will not be Rochester's 'doll', the small, reduced, disempowered object of a man's, a husband's mastering intentions (*Jane Eyre*, vol. 2, ch. 9).

Dolls are not real persons, which is their point. Theoretical modelling reduces texts to the status of the doll, the toy. In Iris Murdoch's fetching phrase, theory, and Theory especially, makes 'small myths, toys, crystals'. The phrase comes in her famous essay 'Against Dryness', which is protesting against most of mid-twentieth-century modernity's philosophy, aesthetics, poetics and cultural practice (modernism, surrealism, post-Kantianism, materialism, existentialism), for thinning our sense of persons and their context, the whole social scene they inhabit: 'far too shallow and flimsy an idea of human personality' was being mongered.[10] Small myths, toys, crystals: dry, tiny, hard. *Mutatis mutandis* she could have been reflecting on Theory's vulgar desires and Theory's vulgar practices, their effort at knowing by diminishing – their map-likeness.

133

To repeat: the model, the map, of their very nature, reduce. They are as it were microstomatic; they speak with a small mouth. This is their necessary mode, their necessary truth. Borges's lovely little story of 1946, *Of Exactitude in Science* (*Del rigor en la ciencia*) — it purports to be a passage from a seventeenth-century travel book — indicates precisely why that smallness has to be, by mocking the zany impracticality of a map which did not select, and the cartographers who exceeded the normative reductiveness, the normal microstomatism of mapping.

> . . . In that Empire, the craft of Cartography attained such Perfection that the Map of a Single province covered the space of an entire City, and the Map of the Empire itself an entire Province. In the course of Time, these extensive maps were found somehow wanting, and so the College of Cartographers evolved a Map of the Empire that was of the same Scale as the Empire and that coincided with it point for point. Less attentive to the Study of Cartography, succeeding Generations came to judge a map of such Magnitude cumbersome, and, not without Irreverence, they abandoned it to the Rigours of sun and Rain. In the western Desert, tattered Fragments of the Map are still to be found, Sheltering an occasional Beast or beggar; in the whole Nation, no other relic is left of the Discipline of Geography.[11]

The map that's one-to-one with what it represents is no use as model. It's just a bad cartographical dream, a mapmaker's folly, and a map reader's nightmare. Such a map would represent the absolute opposite of theorizing, the negative indeed of interpretation, of hermeneutics. It would stand to theory and criticism as the notorious Borges character Pierre Menard — the man who copies out the whole of *Don Quixote* word for word — stands to a real reader of Cervantes's novel. But the truth about the usefulness of the true map, the one that represents by misrepresenting, that cuts reality down to its chosen scale, remains: it means, *per se*, loss — because it depletes the full-scale reality it purports to represent. As all modellers know. The modeller's model aeroplane carries no human cargo. Lilliput stands for Swift's

England, but only as small figure, a catachresis of that reality. Lilliput may represent the truth of Swift's friend Bishop Berkeley and his *Essay Towards a New Theory of Vision* (1709), with its very sound observation that, however hard we try, we can only see, can only take in, a small amount of phenomena at a time – *minima visibilia*. And we do, naturally, have to act upon, to make do, with the *minima* which are all we can perceive at one go. We have to settle precisely for the smallness of our maps, our small models, small though they be. As that bitter sceptic about modelling's power, Thomas Hardy's Sue Bridehead in the novel *Jude the Obscure*, indicates when she attacks a travelling model of Jerusalem for its inaccuracies, its piously conjectural unscholarliness, and then supplies her own counter-model on her school classroom's blackboard. Such truth as there is to be had, will be accessed by some Lilliputian version, despite its minimal visibility. But still the model, however truthful in its minimalist fashion, is not the real thing. And its great asset – precisely this accessible minimality, the dimensional difference that demarcates it from the real it can only signify by this miniaturization – is also its great drawback. Dickens knew this as clearly as Hardy, and so did the novelist Louis-Ferdinand Céline.

In *Bleak House* (chapter 20) the 'elfin' Smallweed, out to lunch with friends, leads the way in selecting from 'the catalogue of viands' at the Slap-Bang eatery. No one can eat everything; a meal, like an interpretation, requires selection; even Jobling, who eats and eats, can't consume the whole menu. The legal trio's food is brought to them by a waitress 'bearing what is apparently a model of the tower of Babel, but what is really a pile of plates and flat tin dish-covers'. For these urbanites, Londoners, London consumers, the Babelic city comes in a figure, in little. The model resembles the tower of Babel, and yet is obviously not it. The likeness is all these men are going to get. It's a revelatory sufficiency – as the food they eat is a sufficing part only of the whole catalogue of viands – but it is never going to grant full knowledge of the whole it represents, of the whole (so to say) urban menu. The Babelic tower of plates certainly represents the tower of Babel, that potent emblem of the City, but only in miniature. Rather like the heap of torn lace waiting to be mended in Céline's mother's shop in the Passage des Bérésines in *Death on the Instalment Plan* (English translation 1938) – that 'pile of Horror'. The pile of cloth encapsulates city truths for Céline; it represents Paris, this version of the tower of Babel in cloth; but it's a merely tiny thing in comparison to what it figures.

London in a pile of plates, Paris in a heap of torn cloth, Jerusalem in a blackboard sketch, Britain as Lilliput, signification in an algorithm $\frac{S}{s}$, all of fiction's functions in a plan of six actants joined up by five arrows, textuality in a word, an apophthegm, reading in a nutshell: the model speaks volumes; the microstoma, the small mouth, shouts aloud – their power a tribute to the real force of metaphor, metonym, synecdoche, the power of the small figure to play big league. Poetry and fiction do it all the time – making the tiny particular, the single image, the shortest story, stand for actualities on the largest scale. It's the force of the tiny that's not unlike the power of the small thought to have enormous scope, to as it were box way beyond its apparent weight, as rhapsodically described in Nicholas Baker's intriguing meditation on *The Size of Thoughts* (1966):

a thought in the presence of which whole urban centers would rise to their feet, and cry out with expressions of gratefulness and kinship; a thought with grandeur, and drenching, barrel-scorning cataracts, and denotations of fist-clenched hope, and hundreds of cellos; a thought that can tear phone-books in half, and rap on the iron nodes of experience until every blue girder rings; a thought that may one day pack everything noble and good into its briefcase, elbow past the curators of purposelessness, travel overnight towards Truth, and shake it by the indifferent marble shoulders until it finally whispers its cool assent – this is the size of thought worth thinking about.

It's a tribute to how the reach of the best of Theory extends beyond itself, a tribute to the encapsulating, summary power of Theory's tiny maps to pack a lot in. But the limitations remain. It's no accident, it seems to me, that Jean Baudrillard, one of Theory's gurus, should define his notion of *simulacra* – basically, the image, or textual object, as the ultimate Theory dream, the imaginative work that 'bears no relation to any reality whatever' – in a rejection of Borges's parable about maps. No longer, Baudrillard claims, do our postmodern models map territories. In his video-nasty postmodernist world, models only generate 'a real without origin or reality: a hyperreal'. So Baudrillard really has to mis-take and reject Borges's parable: its piercing vision of how Theory's models wrong the world by diminishing it is too uncomfortable for him. He wants to embrace guilt-free world-shrinking, to be the happiest of Happy Wanderers of world devastation.[12]

Vladimir Propp, in many ways such an exemplary Theorist, is less openly vastatory than Baudrillard, but is still utterly clear about how theory inevitably leaves things out. The 'number of functions is extremely small', he tells us, 'whereas the number of personages' in Russian stories 'is extremely large'. For Propp, 'this explains the two-fold quality of a tale': on the one hand 'its amazing multiformity, picturesqueness, and colour, and on the other its no less striking uniformity, its repetition'. His theorizing work makes no bones about going in for the recursiveness of the thirty-one functions, and not dwelling on the amazing multiformity, picturesqueness and colour he knows is also there. But this is purchasing knowledge at great expense – by neglect of what larger-minded reading cannot neglect. It is no accident that it is precisely the amazing multiformity, picturesqueness and colour of a fiction that draws in non-theorizing readers, even when they are well aware of the extremely recursive, repetitive nature of any particular fiction they happen to be reading. Another Michael Dibdin, or Stephen King, another Iris Murdoch, even another Henry James, may, indeed will, greatly resemble the last one of theirs that you read, and will, naturally, have lots in common also with the genre it represents, and with the bourgeois Western novel, and the Novel, and prose narrative, even with Literature itself. But it's what this author is doing this time that matters, as much as, if not more than, what he or she did last time, and that, certainly, matters far more than its kinships, its family likenesses with its mode, its genres, its formal kind. And that's what Theory's abstractions are, by their partiality, their necessary partiality, leaving out of the account. For Propp, all the heroes of the tales he analyses are motivated, he finds, by the realization of a lack. What he doesn't realize is that his Theory's lack of interest in the particularities of the personae whom he paints only in their formalistic and functional colours, is a lack too far, driving negatively as this neglect does at the heart of what actually motivates readers to read on.

Lévi-Strauss's waspishness about Propp's Formalism is instructive. It destroys, says Lévi-Strauss, the fictions it analyses because of its lacks. This 'Formalism destroys its object', because its analysis is confined only to the syntax, the syntagmatic level; it's interested only in a morphological, a syntactical, a grammatical model of story. Its analytic or theoretical map is thus crucially limited. This mapping leaves out the lexical level; it refuses to operate a vocabulary model. This is then the error of Propp's Formalism: 'the belief that the grammar can be tackled at once and the dictionary postponed. But what is true for some linguistic systems is even more true for myths and tales. This is so because in this case grammar and vocabulary are not only closely linked while operating at distinct levels; they virtually adhere to each other on all surfaces and cover each other completely'.

This is a devastating critique of Propp, but also of any theorizing, any model-building, which leaves elements out for the sake of the model's necessary clarity, the map's necessary legibility, choosing for the sake of analysis (as Theory perpetually does) to postpone consideration of things – beginning of course with Saussure's foundational waivings of signifieds, diachrony and *parole* – which cannot however be postponed for ever. Such dissociations of what, finally, cannot be dissociated – and Theory is the great dissociator – are utterly detrimental to the analysis, the Theory in effect, being propounded.

By restricting itself exclusively to the rules which govern the grouping of propositions, [Formalism erroneously] loses sight of the fact that no language exists in which the vocabulary can be deduced from the syntax. The study of any linguistic system requires the cooperation of the grammarian and the philologist. This means that in the matter of oral tradition the morphology is sterile unless direct or indirect ethnographic observation comes in to render it fertile. Imagining that the two tasks can be dissociated, that the grammatical study can be undertaken first and the lexical study postponed until later, one is condemned to produce nothing but an anemic grammar and lexicon in which anecdotes replace definitions. In the end, neither would accomplish its purpose.[13]

Sterility, anaemia, failure of purpose on every side: the narrowing effects of Propp's analysis could scarcely be more devastatingly put. Morphology alone will not do. And the barrenness of Propp's morphologizings stand, I'm suggesting, for Theory's general habit of binding and bounding, its limited descriptions, its earnest limitings of the force, the meaning, the effects and affects of writing, its thinnings and prunings of the large field of literary phenomena, and of the individual texts, the epiphenomena within that huge, unbounded field. Reading, real reading, proper reading, cries out for more, much more.

9

Touching Reading

Somewhere, everywhere, now hidden, now apparent in whatever is written down is the form of a human being.

Virginia Woolf, 'Reading'

The dust of Theory settles and, as Italo Calvino describes it, the classic
is still being read. 'A classic', he says, for his Eighth Definition of one,
'is a work which constantly generates a pulviscular cloud of critical
discourse around it, but which always shakes the particles off'. The
classic remains, after all criticism, all Theory, still to be read. On this
view the dust of Theory has to be shaken off before the reading of the
classic can continue.[1] And I agree to the extent of saying that reading
can only proceed effectively, properly, truly, when much of what
Theory alleges and Theory gets up or has got up to, is left behind.
Reading needs to go transalpine, beyond Theory, to cross Theory's
Alps, or its Pyrenees, those High Pyrrhonisms Theory has thrown up
around texts and the reading experience. Theory's Pyrrhonisms break
up the reading relationship – get in the way of the respect for the
otherness of the other person and the other person's text, which in Iris
Murdoch's compelling vision is the only ground of a fruitful relationship, because it's the only ground of love, is the only ethicity. Murdoch's
husband John Bayley, now her widower, put this very nicely in calling the characters of great fictions *The Characters of Love* (his title of
1960). Great fiction arises, both Murdoch and Bayley agree, in a relationship of respect for otherness – the author letting 'others be through
him', in Murdoch's demanding formula. This is love; it is also, of

140

course, forgiveness. Theory, as we've seen, will have none of this: its procedures are based in thoroughgoing disrespect for the otherness of the author and his/her text. Theory suspects, bypasses, smothers, overcomes, belittles authors and texts. It doesn't forgive.

Not a theorist of a postmodern disposition, John Keats talked in his astonishing sonnet 'On Sitting Down to Read King Lear Once Again' of having 'once more' to 'humbly assay' Shakespeare's play. To *assay* it, to weigh its worth, like an assayer testing a lump of ore for its content of precious metal, or measuring the fineness of a piece of gold or silver; and doing so humbly, as in the presence of something finer than himself which demands respect, subservience even, as from the lesser poetic practitioner opening the pages of *il miglior fabbro* ('the greater maker', to quote T. S. Eliot's tribute to Ezra Pound in dedicating *The Waste Land* to him). In great contrast, the Theorist proudly scorns and cheerfully rewrites. No masterful masterpieces for him or her; only another occasion for strutting their Theoretical stuff, for mastering the piece in question. And I know which posture seems apter to the case of reading great writing – which one in fact respects more the human contract which reading of any literature really involves, the human relationship Theory has done its very best to deny and obliterate.

Theory's Pyrrhonisms did not only dehumanize texts, and not least by denying them a humanizing link to authors, they dehumanized readers and reading in the same fell swoop. Propp's functions are *of course* less numerous than the personae of the tales he examines, and registering functions requires less human interest than encountering personae. Propp's morphologizings, to put it bluntly, hollow out the human interest of the reading engagement. And in so doing they stand for so much of the dehumanizing cast of Theory's belittlements and inducements. It's no surprise if I the reader am belittled when the text is. The unforgiving exclusionist politics of Theory, grounded in Saussureanism's exclusions and waivings of history and *parole*, will exclude readers who do not fit the model's mould. Read as we say, or don't read at all. But what if I am not so simply definable as one of Theory's allowed readers – a disempowered one, a Woman, a Black, and so on? What if I'm a WEM, a white European male, theory's Public Enemy Number 2 (Number 1 is the *Dead* WEM)? What if, as I believe to be more commonly the case, I'm a funny *mélange* of Theory's approved and disapproved, moving in and out of desired and undesirable categories or 'communities', as they say – as I do: a male, a father, a Christian, a don in elitist Oxford, but also a socialist, a republican, a holder of an Irish passport? I don't read very well As A Woman (hard though I try), but I do read as a member of a still colonized tribe, though also as a *Protestant* member of it. I don't think Theory's exclusionist visions allow very well for my personal paradoxes and striated allegiances. But then they don't allow for so many human varieties, even if they bang on all the time about difference and its glories. One of the very good points Catharine Stimpson makes is that the much bandied-about category 'woman' is itself just too impossibly unfitting for the realities of woman-reader varieties (women writers 'are more than women. They belong to many "writing communities" at once').[2]

But then the human has been at the very heart of Theory's attacks upon authors and reference and logocentrism. Humanism and the subject – the 'subject' considered as both human being so to say in the street, and as human object of attention in a writing – became dirty words, outlawed interests, deplored literary connections in Theory's heyday, allowed in only to be jeered at, considered viable only as old-fashioned concerns now all undone, unravelling, 'decentred'. This depreciation, this subjugation, this blanking out could not, of course, be sustained. Even in Theory's heyday there was resistance to this rhetoric, and so there should have been, and so there should be now. And if there is one feature of what reading should do and engage with, and yes, theorize, 'after' Theory, it is the presence, the rights, the needs of the human subject, in texts, in the originations of texts, in the reception of texts. It was, I'm happy to observe, never easy for that old human centre to be so briskly decentred by Theory, to keep the negative place assigned it, to keep its allotted blankness blank. And the human did make its way steadily back in, *sub rosa* often, but still there was a return of the human repressed, as authors insisted on being still alive and kicking, and human subjects just would not quit the critical stage, would not accept their defacings and depersonifyings, and human subjects in the shape of real readers as well as of recognizably human characters with more or less centred selves went on featuring in fictions and being featured in readings of fictions.

And this isn't simply a matter of following the tricky logics of deconstruction, and reading negatives as positives – recognizing that the human subject was really present in and through all of its negativizing by Theorists, like saying that Jews were really being granted their due cultural importance by being featured in Paul de Man's anti-semitic articles (a common deconstructionist move), or that the widespread deciding that texts were utterly undecidable was itself a profound recognition all round of textual decidability (as Michael Riffaterre has done).[3] Though there is something in such a mode of approaching and seeing through Theory's great negativity about the old human contract of reading. The intrusive presence of the Theorist, for example, insisting on staging herself as a reader, pushily shoving himself into the forefront of the scene of reading, was of course a declaration of human identity, of the necessity of the human subject in the reading act and of human contact with the interpreted text. Even the grimmer exclusions and demarcations of politicized reading – of what Ihab Hassan wittily dubbed Reading According to GRIM, the Great Rumbling Ideological Machine[4] – were done in the name of real readers with real human sensibilities on the Gender Race and Class front (as in Lisa Jardine's notoriously brisk eviction of Philip Larkin from her syllabus at Queen Mary College, in London's East End, because the students 'down my way', being mainly black and female and working class, were not to be expected to stomach his porno-misogynist white-man elitisms).[5]

Nor did the return of the human have to wait on the shock of the Paul de Man affair – though that did have the enormously salutary effect of bringing his pupils and fans greatly to their senses about matters of history and reference in texts, and it did mightily spur on the enormous turn, especially in the USA, to the subject of the Shoah, to the texts of Holocaust memory, and the whole business of literature as

143

an archive of the human, especially as an affair of memory, of elegiac recall and celebration. (One moment, so to say, Shoshana Felman is defending her Master on the grounds that he taught that history and reference don't matter in texts, and the next she's having loud second thoughts and sharing in the volume *Testimony: Crises of Witnessing in Literature*, albeit very grudgingly with another attempt to whitewash Paul de Man, this time by arguing that when he wrestled with Benjamin wrestling with the 'impossibility' of the task of the translator and 'Benjamin's articulation of a radical articulateness of contemporary history', he was bearing witness 'historically' – with no worrying at all, of course, about de Man's misreading of Benjamin's *Aufgabe* – but still accepting the existence of personal and historical presences in writing.)[6] The return of the historically real human subject had already begun, even before that moment of deconstruction's truly tragic reversal, its *peripateia*, when hubristic soaring was brought low by true *anagnorisis*, by belated recognition of where the Theory leader was coming from and what his Theory's suppression of history really amounted to by way of personal covering up of the historical tracks.

Obviously, the fine somatic preoccupations of Michel Foucault, spreading everywhere, helped: you can't have an interest in bodies and what power does to them without an interest, a truly human interest, in the human owners of those bodies. (And the vast range of Body interests in current criticism, historiography, Cultural Studies, and so on – there's scarcely a museum in any part of the globe which hasn't had, or is about to have, a major exhibition about the representation of bodiliness, anatomy, medical practices – indicates not just the massive generative force of Foucault's analyses but the widespread emphatic return of interest in the human subject.) And Jacques Derrida was protesting almost from the start of the mid-1960s US interest in his deconstructionist analyses that he was being misconstrued as being hostile to presence and history and the human (why he was not listened to is one of the most arresting clues to the depth of the implanted ideological need in the US academy to resist precisely those things: a matter of the politics of post-Second World War academic and intellectual life still needing analysis and interpretation). And

Roland Barthes's move beyond a purely formalistic structuralism into a poststructuralist embracing of the human world began almost as soon as he became renowned in the anglophone world for being a high formalist. The narrative codes of *S/Z* were soon letting in – and how could they in all truth not? – the context of the text, what Barthes called 'the cultural codes' of a text, which had to do with the types of knowledge a text might yield: physical, physiological, medical, psychological, historical, as well as literary.[7] And before long the purist–structuralist waivers of the authorial, the historical, the ethnological, and the kerygmatic (all those features carefully not discussed in Barthes's symptomatic structuralist piece 'The Struggle With the Angel')[8] had all but disappeared, as Barthes the critic foregrounded himself as reader and subject in *Barthes par Barthes* (sandals, non-beetroot-strewn roads of southern France, and all), as a writer the grain of whose voice, *Le Grain de la voix*, precisely mattered in the reading business, and promoted a view of writing as the container of human content, especially the matters of body, pain, grief, desire, mourning and memory.[9] The real absence of loved and desired ones came to sum up, as it were, the desired presence of the absent, the dead, in texts generally (and not just in the photographic texts of *Camera Lucida*), came to represent that flawed reality of the presence of the human in texts, a presence made tangible especially when the body and the self were *punctured*, as Barthes has it, by pleasure, by pain, and by grief. The *punctum*, the grievous piercings *Camera Lucida* discusses, the reality of the hole in the self when it's afflicted by loss and its attendant emotions, became utterly central to Barthes not only as realities of life, of the flesh, of the body he inhabited, but also as allegories of reading, of the meaning of texts, as much in (the sadism-inflected) *Sade/Fourier/Loyola* as in *Camera Lucida*.[10] The question of mourning, and its grand related thematic of the text as archive of old, long-gone things and also, more crucially, as elegy, as writing engaged in the emotionality of grief and loss and in the fraught, questionable desire to have the lost one made present once more, brought back again in a writing ('Weep no more, woeful shepherds weep no more, / For Lycidas your sorrow is not dead'): such issues clearly became more central to Derrida upon the death of

Paul de Man. But Derrida's interest in the textuality of mourning clearly runs far more widely than just that evidently most moving of losses, and engages with Derrida's long interest in loss and absence and annihilation as a Jew, a child of the Holocaust years, and as a person maturing under the threat of nuclear annihilation. Such realities of grief and loss and memory are clearly fundamental to, as they provide analogues of, all the reading-subjects which have preoccupied Derrida's critical attention through the later deconstructionist decades: friendship, law, testimony, the gift, hospitality, religion, cosmopolitanism, forgiveness, the death penalty, and so on. Of course, these analyses keep running, as one might predict, along the old lines of deconstruction's favoured binarism – the *two interpretations* of whatever is at hand – where the old Saussurean doublenesses are locked indissolubly together in an *aporia* of positive and negative – each *indissoluble from the other* and both also *irreducible to each other*, in the double-bind which became Derrida's analytical trademark.[11]

But whatever the Theory-led hesitations in that Derridean hovering, the practical fact of the reading matter is that his reading is being performed and is being presented as to be done, as an affair which includes historical and political reference and also offers an emotional and ethical engagement. Something similar can be said of the great politicization that has gone on within the broad frame of the linguistic turn. And I would like to think that these human connections of the textual are inescapable. The Theorist in Derrida is of course hesitant about any positive content – not unlike Roland Barthes in, say, the preface to *Sade/Fourier/Loyola*, refusing the old notion of open access to meaning, to 'message', to what he calls the old-fashioned guarantees of textual truth, 'socialism, faith, evil', 'social responsibility', the old ethical purposefulness of reading and writing. But what Derrida calls 'concrete history', the concreteness of readers concretely in and being placed in their history, their political situation, their ethicity, their emotionality, simply refuses to be shaken off, or out – as Roland Barthes cannot help (as I'd like to think) holding that 'the pleasure of the Text also includes the amicable return of the author', the author as a body, and the reader too as a body and an emotionality or self inevitably caught up in 'bourgeois ideology'. A self defined by current politics and ethics, by current 'determinations, visions, projections', keen on 'messages', and who must 'listen to the message's transport', to its pleasures, its emotional charge.

The caveats and reluctances imposed by Theory are utterly clear in these cases, but also clear is the persistence of an ancient reading pro-gramme, in which the best kind of reading is envisaged as a complex affair of whole-person engagement with the text. It begins, as might be expected, in bodily contact, in close reading in a physical sense. Like Czeslaw Milosz in his impressive poem 'Readings' – about read-ing the gospels in Greek and finding there truths about the twentieth-century's demonizations – as the reader turns the text which he touches, his finger moving along the line of the words on the page, into words forming in his mouth.

> You asked me what is the good of reading the Gospels in Greek.
> I answer that it is proper that we move our finger
> Along letters more enduring than those carved in stone,
> And that, slowly pronouncing each syllable,
> We discover the true dignity of speech.[12]

The reading begins in close bodily contact, which turns into close mental and emotional contact with text, a sequence of contacts in which the reading result is a scene of complex whole-person ethical instruction, deeply rooted in rationality but particularly in emotional-ity. This is a reading outcome close to what Aristotle and the Renais-sance critics who followed him were trying to specify as katharsis – a purging of the emotional self, a kind of ethical invigoration through engagement with the emotional highs and lows of tragedy. What Martha Nussbaum nicely glosses in 'Interlude 2: luck and tragic emotions' in her greatly instructive book *The Fragility of Goodness*, as the ethical effect contingent upon the emotional affect of Greek tragedy.[13]

Seeing the reading transaction as something like this – the affect–

effect as ethics, the ethical result as a law of reading – is undoubtedly what induced the Christian tradition to keep invoking the sacramental or eucharistic model. 'Take, eat: this is my [textual] body, which is broken for you: this do in remembrance of me. For as often as ye eat this bread, and drink this cup, ye do shew forth the Lord's death' (1 Corinthians 11). Here's a body of text, and the text as body, the body of the other, the text as other, to be consumed, ingested, in a memorial act, an act of personal reception and reflection, an inward event which is also an outward-facing act, an act of testimony, of worldly witness – something with an invisible but also a visible effect; a sharing of signs, a mutual signifying system, in which signs are given, received, taken up and in, and also made manifest, especially in the results for the recipient. In this sacrament, this holy communion, the believer is blessed and graced, signed as Christ's own, marked as sanctified. In reading on this model, the reader is, in some way or another, also graced, blessed, marked as the text's own.

The Judaeo-Christian tradition dwells constantly on the sweetness of the Word of God. The words of Jehovah in the Psalms are frequently sweet ones, like honey in the mouth. Gerard Manley Hopkins talks in his poem 'Felix Randal' of the 'sweet reprieve' of the eucharist. Here at the Table of the Lord is pleasing eating, pleasant nourishment, or at least eating with a taste you can savour, sweet or not. Keats rightly tastes, in *King Lear*, 'the bittersweet of this Shakespearian fruit'. For Graham Greene's Scobie in *The Heart of the Matter* (1948), taking the eucharist in a state of mortal sin, the wafer is 'the pale papery taste of his eternal sentence on his tongue'. But the point is that for reading on this model there is always something to taste, something definite and defining to take in. *Crede et manducasti* is the Augustinian conception: believe and you take into your person food for the soul. The Word of God, the body of Christ, become you: to your emotional, ethical, spiritual benefit. And so it is with all reading where this model of reading as a selving, self-making process has prevailed. On this plan the words of the text that you seriously and closely engage with become you, get into you, have personal effect. Which is why Coleridge can fancy himself as having in him a smack of Prince Hamlet; why

T. S. Eliot's Prufrock can try out literary models on himself (Prince Hamlet? Attendant Lord? Fool?); why Harold Bloom extols becoming what you read (ingest the poem, memorize it, become it);[14] why Italo Calvino defines the classic as the book that becomes you, which turns into you because it has got so far into you. '"Your" classic is a book . . . which helps you define yourself in relation or even in opposition to it.'[15] Emily Dickinson, Bloom tells us in *How to Read*, 'read the Bible pretty much as she read Shakespeare and Dickens, in search of characters she could absorb into her own drama'. She was not alone in this; such absorption was utterly normative once upon a time; and so it should be now. It is of course what the potent Gadamerian idea of the reader's horizons converging with the horizons of the text is, *inter alia*, about.[16]

These are traditional notions and assumptions which Theory deliberately — at least in theory — estranged itself from. And it's true that some of the stronger Prufrockian claims by readers to have become characters in fiction — Coleridge's fancy that he had that smack of Hamlet in him, or Bloom's belief that he's Falstaff, and the like[17] — will always have a smack of the merely self-puffing fantastic about them. But not thinking that something like this can and should happen depletes the idea of reading. Martha Nussbaum is right to deplore the way Theorists simply ignored the work not just of moral philosophers but of moral philosophers with an intense interest in literature, and not least Iris Murdoch. Astonishingly, Theory has refused even to notice what Iris Murdoch had to suggest about the ethical force of literature, her powerful cluster of arguments, coming not only from a powerfully practising novelist, but also from a well-read moral philosopher — those arguments of Murdoch's that the novelist is an exemplary 'good man' when at his best his fictions offer 'free' characters built out of respect for 'the otherness of the other person', which is Murdoch's definition of goodness in persons generally and not just in novelists; and her case that when this morality is in place in a fiction then literature is 'a case of morals', exemplarily moral, instructively moral.[18] It is indeed an astonishing overlooking, part, as Nussbaum suggests, of the way Theory blotted out the once standard assumption that literature was about human behaviour and preoccupied with questions of how to live, presentations which inevitably provide mirrors for the real living of their readers. As Nussbaum puts it, echoing Murdoch, literature is a kind of moral philosophy and theories of reading which respected and valued literature as ethically and emotionally educative were sound ones whose obscuration wrongs literature.[19] If personal interaction, some such personal contact, does not occur, then the reading act is, I would agree, crucially impaired. Recovering some such from the gulag archipelago Theory would banish it to is utterly necessary.

As I say, it has been hard for reading practices to live up to Theory's self-denials, and the ethical–emotional affect–effect has, in one way or another, managed to return in order to put Theory's abstinences in these regards to shame. But this is ground which still needs claiming, and reclaiming, openly, not covertly, or accidentally, or shamefacedly, and not in any qualified, half-hearted, late-deconstructionist fashion either. The reclamation is justified not least by its support by every scene of reading I can think of, in literature as well as in history. Fiction cries out, on every hand, to be taken this way: as Martha Nussbaum has potently pointed out in her readings of Henry James's novels as being all about induction into an ethical maturity, commanded by the need – illustrated, made known, shown to be of the essence – for great sensitivity of regard, of perception, in the reading response.

The scenes of reading which James stages again and again, finely model this educative, heuristic reading process in vividly illustrating it. Strether's encounter with Chad and Madame de Vionnet, for instance, in *The Ambassadors* (1902; Bk 11, chs 3 and 4 in the New York edition) is justly famed as one of the finest examples of these instructive encounters, but it is also merely characteristic of many such. Strether, out for the day in the French countryside, waiting for his supper at a riverside auberge, sees a young couple approaching in a rowing-boat; he's shocked to realize that they're his American friend Chad and his French friend Mme de Vionnet; he notices their consternation; and their intimacy gradually dawns on him – an intimacy they are not going to own up to in so many words. The realization is a blow to Strether's puritanism, but a main element in his long journey of moral readjustment and education that his journey to France is compelling him into. James's slow run-up to the crisis moment of vision emphasizes the encounter's role as an allegory of reading. Earlier, Strether had felt that his day's rural rambling was contained within the frame, as it were, of a painting by Lambinet that he was moved by at a Boston dealer's. He 'was freely walking about in it'. He's reminded too of a story by Maupassant. He feels himself altogether in 'a land of fancy'; feels he's at a play, watching, indeed at, or on, 'a scene and a stage'; he's aware of being in 'a text', feels there's 'not a breath of the cooler evening' that isn't 'somehow a syllable of the text'. In other words he's in, and present at, a drama, a fiction, as participant and also as observer, reader, theorist. Strether reads slowly, but he reads impressively. Chad and Mme de Vionnet 'present themselves . . . clearly'. The 'air' is 'thick' with 'intimations'. Strether has a 'sense' of things; he 'takes in' things; he takes in that he knows the woman. He becomes aware; he sees. He doesn't realize the fullness of the scene's meanings straight away. That takes reflection (favourite Jamesian word and activity). But as he reflects, 'later on and in private', puts an interpretative squeeze on the impressions he's been touched by, as he meditates on them, 'many things . . . as it were, fitted together'. There is a fullness of meaning to be had by meditation. Back at his hotel, 'He was, at that point of vantage, in full possession, to make of it all he could'. This making is, as ever with James, a making out, a process of discovery, of finding, of seeing clearly what was there; which is also a kind of invention, a making up, a telling of a story of interpretation. But it is a fullness; and a moral fullness. 'He kept making of it that there had been simply *a lie* in the charming affair – a lie on which one could now, detached and deliberate, perfectly put one's finger.' The 'deep, deep truth of the intimacy' is thus 'revealed'. A lie, the truth: this is reading for knowledge, and moral knowledge, acquired through moral and emotional shock dwelt on, meditated on, absorbed.

It comes only slowly, by protracted hands-on engagement with the arresting textual scene – James even uses what is for him the terribly violent metaphor of *gouging*. Strether has got to use his fingernails, metaphorically, to scrape away at the scene's meaning. He 'gouged deeper into the matter'. But the gouging works, works at the level of character. Strether is stretched morally; his hermeneutics is a moralized, moralizing, ethically strenuous one. And there's intense ethical reciprocity in the encounter. Strether is morally engaged and changed by it, and so are Chad and Mme de Vionnet. As Strether reads them, so they read him. The meeting of interpretative horizons is mutually transforming. Nothing will ever be the same again, for these people, but especially for Strether, James's example of a reader. And though there is manifest shock, and surprise, and suggestions of farcicality ('Queer as fiction, as farce'), and complete realization of the couple's lie and so of the truth of the case only comes gradually, come it does. There is a slow movement towards realization, meaning, truth, a transformative ethical result. On this view, reading is more hesitant than hasty; it requires a certain effortful gouging out; but there is, in the end, no final *aporia*. This is reading, hermeneutic, epistemology, beyond *aporia*.

And so it is with other scenes of reading staged by literature and history, not least with those readers I began with, Robinson Crusoe reading the Bible as the road to salvation, and Maggie Tulliver reading herself into a condition of renunciation in the pages of Thomas à Kempis. The words on the page turn into words *for them*.

> I daily read the Word of God, and apply'd all the Comforts of it to my present State: One Morning being very sad, I open'd the Bible upon these Words, *I will never, never leave thee, nor forsake thee*; immediately it occurr'd, That these Words were to me, Why else should they be directed in such a Manner, just at the Moment when I was mourning over my Condition, as one forsaken of God and Man?[20]

Thus Crusoe. And so it goes with other classic readers from classic fiction. With little Jane Eyre, for instance. We are introduced to her in the introductory pages of *Jane Eyre* as she reads 'certain introductory pages' in Bewick's *History of British Birds,* and finds in Bewick's words and pictures featuring lonely seabirds in icy northern landscapes, mirrors of her own orphaned unhappiness as a scarcely welcomed guest in her aunt's house. 'Of these death-white realms I formed an idea of my own.' 'Each picture told a story; mysterious often to my undeveloped understanding and imperfect feelings, yet ever profoundly interesting: as interesting as the tales' the servant Bessie would sometimes narrate, feeding 'our eager attention with passages of love and adventure taken from old fairy tales and older ballads; or (as at a later period I discovered) from the pages of *Pamela,* and *Henry, Earl of Moreland.*' Reading like this is for pleasure, often those curiously painful pleasures existing in the 'beyond' of Freud's wry 'pleasure principle'. It is also for knowledge. And above all it's for a kind of self-knowledge, an education in understanding and feeling one's own condition. It's a sentimental education. It's a kind of self-arming too. When Jane's fat cousin stops her from reading his book (all the books '*are* mine') and throws it at her, causing her to bang her head on the door as she dodges the missile, she knows how to define his cruelty. 'You are like a murderer – you are like a slave-driver – you are like the Roman emperors!' Reading has given her, in the words of the late Marie Cardinale, *The Words to Say It.* 'I had read *Goldsmith's History of Rome,* and had formed my opinion of Nero, Caligula, &c. Also I had drawn parallels in silence, which I never thought thus to have declared aloud.' Opinion formed in the private space of reading, parallels drawn in the silence of reading assimilation, have given her access to publicly available meanings and interpretations. Her words do get her into trouble. Cousin John throws himself at her, pulls her hair, calls her a rat; they fight; she is locked up in the Red Room for being such a 'picture of passion'. But there is no gainsaying the aptness of what she has learned from her books.

To be sure, such classic places of meditation on the positive outcomes of reading do acknowledge that there can be misinterpretation, misreading. There is even a very Derridean sense on these occasions, at these self-reflexive metatextual moments, that useful reading, helpful reading, can only occur, can only be envisaged, where the possibility of misreading also exists. 'Take heed / Of mis-interpreting; for that, instead / Of doing good, will but thyself abuse: / By mis-interpreting, evil insues.' Thus the concluding poem at the end of Bunyan's *The Pilgrim's Progress* (1678–84), a narrative which is an extended demonstration of the dual possibility of getting the Bible right, but also getting it wrong. Those heavy Calvinist male Bible readers in *Jane Eyre*, the Revd Mr Brocklehurst and the missionary St John Rivers, are offered as examples precisely of Bible misreading utterly disconcerting to true Bible readers, Jane herself and her friend Helen Burns. But unlike with our vulgar Theorists, there is no jumping to any conclusion on these occasions that no truthful, no positively educative reading, no usefully determinate reading, is possible just because there's a distinct possibility of uncertainty and multivalence, even of *aporia*.

> Put by the Curtains, look within my Veil;
> Turn up my Metaphors, and do not fail
> There, if thou seekest them, such things to find,
> As will be helpful to an honest mind.

So John Bunyan's concluding poem goes on. Beyond, behind, through the veil of Bunyan's allegory, his metaphoricity, there are helpful things to be found; but only to the honest seeker, the reader prepared ethically for the ethical encounter. What's on offer is a most personal encounter based in a kind of ethical law of reading.

> Boswell's turbulent friend
> And his deafening verbal strife,
> Ivan Ilych's death
> Tell me more about life,
> The meaning and the end
> Of our familiar breath,
> Both being personal,
> Than all the carnage can . . .

154

That's the Scottish poet Edwin Muir in his poem 'Reading in Wartime'.[21] The personal in the text speaks to the person of the reader of those texts; but only on, as it were, Bunyan's terms. There is a law which the revelation offered by Bunyan and claimed by Muir both depend on. Bunyan calls it honesty. Iris Murdoch calls it love – respect for the otherness of the other person, for the personality which Muir recognizes in the texts he finds so telling. I call it tact. Tact: the missing element in Theory's misconstruings and misreadings, in precisely its tactile failures, its mishandlings of text and textuality.

Tact: gentle touch, caring touch, loving touch; appropriate handling, unmanipulative reading. The touch emblematized in Czeslaw Milosz's finger moving along the line of his Greek New Testament. Theory keeps mishandling. Theorists mishandle. They don't care for the sacramental model, not least, I guess, because the sacramental effects of the eucharist are contingent upon the sacred items, the bread, the wine, being sacrally, carefully, perceptively handled, handled with scrupulous regard, 'discerning the Lord's body', as St Paul has it. A careful *attention* (that attitude of the religious, described thus by Simone Weil, which so attracts Iris Murdoch) manifest in the communicant's clean hands, reflective of a 'clean' heart, hands which respect what's offered, which don't pollute or snatch, or otherwise abuse the sacred object that is to be piously ingested.

The long history of serious reflection on the behaviour of believers and ministers at the holy communion table or altar is mightily preoccupied with what their hands do as the sacred bread is offered and received. These discussions are full of horror at the possibility of misappropriation, of mis-taking. Some of Milton's harshest Puritan satirical scorn in his tracts *Of Reformation Touching Church-Discipline in England: and the Causes that hitherto have hinderd it* (1641) is heaped on romanizing clergy who rail-off the table of communion, debarring the Lord's people from close access to the Lord's body in the bread and wine – 'to keep off the profane touch of the laicks', the touch deemed profane only by bad clerics, 'whilst the obscene, and surfeted Priest scruples not to paw, and mammock the sacramentall bread, as familiarly as his Tavern Bisket'.[22] The Lord's people need a close touch;

the fat priest needs to discern the difference between the sacred bread and his tavern biscuit. Bad hands are getting in the way of true communion and true communicants.

What's wrong with the communicants in T. S. Eliot's 1920 poem 'Gerontion' is that they have the wrong and wronging hands. Christ comes in the 'juvescence of the year', 'To be eaten, to be divided, to be drunk among / whispers'. But Mr Silvero's 'caressing hands' (too mercantile?), Hakagaswa's hands pressed together as he bows (he worships art, the Titians he bows among), Madame de Tornquist's candle-shifting hands (she's preparing for a séance in 'the dark room': demonic raisings of the dead forbidden by Judaeo-Christian orthodoxy), and Fräulein von Kulp's hand on the doorknob of her room (some culpatory sexual invitation afoot?), will not do. These are all bad receivers of the Word, 'The word within a word unable to speak a word' – unable to speak to *them*, its bad handlers. What's missing is in fact tact, in every sense.

Tact: proper tactility; the gentle touch of the right-minded communicant. Tact as proper behaviours before the tended, the offered sacrament; tact as due attention, a proper attending to; a tenderness of touch; tender attention. Tact as that approach with the right hands, the attentively tendered hand of the attentive body, of the body tending towards, the body approaching near, coming carefully close up to the object to be received. The touch that will result in the toucher being touched, in the sense of emotionality, affect. Close reading, no less. The tender, tending, tenting touch of the rightly tactful communicant. The lover.

> So kiss good turtles, so devoutly nice
> As priests in handling reverent sacrifice
> And such in searching wounds the surgeon is
> As we when we embrace or touch or kiss.

Thus John Donne in his *Elegy* 8, Donne who knew a thing or two about delicate and indelicate body contacts, linking the devoted contacts of lovers' bodies with the reverent handling of reverent priests and the careful searching of a wound by a surgeon, tenting instrument in hand. A collusion of unclumsy hands, of truly religious hands. Nothing like the Theorist's hands, abusive on principle. Delivering the low blow Roland Barthes actually celebrates in his essay on wrestling in *Mythologies*, the trickster punch of the pansy wrestler Thauvin, the *salope*, and of Jacob's divine antagonist in Barthes's analysis of the Wrestling Jacob story.[23] True readers don't paw and mammock, don't abuse, the text. True readers are tactful. D. H. Lawrence famously said that morality in the novel was that 'delicate, for ever trembling and changing *balance* between me and my whole circumambient universe', and that this moral balance was only maintained if the novelist did not put 'his thumb in the scale to pull down the balance to his own predilection', which 'is immorality'.[24] And so it is with reading. Tact means not having clumsy thumbs; and Theorists have clumsy thumbs. Theory is very often the clumsy thumb of reading. Stanley Fish once declared himself in favour of 'rules of thumb', rather than rules, when it came to the theorizing of reading.[25] Too much Theory is ruled by the rule of the clumsy thumb. The grossly tactless touch.

It should come, then, as no surprise that Theorists show themselves spectacularly clumsy, as failing dreadfully in the tact, the care, the attention, the lack of which is precisely what Theory's unclose, its distant, railed-off reading, its solipsistic stock-notion ridden practice, repeatedly manifests; no surprise that Theorists should show themselves at their characteristic tactless worst when it comes to handling texts which are in fact about hands, handling, touching, touch.

Much of *Great Expectations* is about hands – hands as markers of class (Pip's little blacksmith's hands, Joe Gargery's big blacksmith's hands – workers' hands Estella makes Pip ashamed of); hands as witnesses to bourgeois horrors about unclean workers, criminals, convicts (the convict Magwitch's 'large brown veinous hands', the convict moll Molly's extraordinarily powerful wrist; lawyer Jaggers's obsessive hand-washing, his 'scraping of the filth of Newgate out of his finger-nails'; and so on). The novel's social–personal–moral sign-system is a detailed semiotic of hands. And Theorists' readings of *Great Expectations* are rightly preoccupied with this Dickensian handiwork.

But how tactlessly, how excruciatingly mistaking is William A. Cohen's handling of 'Manual Conduct in *Great Expectations*'. Hands are up to no good, according to his vision of repressed Victorianism – or they would be if Dickens weren't repressing his desire to let the great masturbatory secret out of the bag and so weren't talking only a hintful obliquity. Pip cannot easily ring Miss Havisham's door-bell, 'on account of the stiff long fingers of my gloves'. Which is a 'manual erection' coinciding with Pip's 'rising expectations', which are about to take the form of a 'sexualized humiliation'. All of the novel's interest in male handshaking is a form of repressed male homosexual encounter. So is the novel's boxing, its punch-ups between boys. Lawyer Jaggers, the hand-washer, bites the forefinger of his large right-hand and puts the left one into his pocket – so he's got one finger in the mouth, signifying fellatio (but no, he hasn't: you don't usually bite your finger by sucking on it, and neither action needs inserting phallicly into the mouth), and the hand in the pocket of course signifies masturbation, the 'bulging' 'secret' of erections.

And Magwitch's propensity to touch Pip, manifest from their first meeting on the Marshes when he holds the lad upside down and empties his pockets (pockets, ah . . .) 'embodies a certain pedophilia' (a *certain* paedophilia: well, is it paedophilia or not?). It's a 'lecherous pawing'. When Magwitch, back from Australia, comes up the stairs of Pip's digs and holds out his hands to the repelled and repelling Pip, kisses Pip's hands, lays a hand on Pip's shoulder, and so on, this is 'the climax of the touching' begun in childhood, now 'in the form of an erotic ballet performed by the hands'. 'This narration', says Cohen, 'has a perilously overt sexual charge'. Which seems to mean it's really about Magwitch's desire to have sex with Pip – a desire manifest for this truly tactless reader from the start of the novel – and that Pip is the object of Magwitch's continuing paedophile lust. Well, that scarcely fits the novel the rest of us have read. Nor is Pip's friend Herbert Pocket (Pocket . . .) immune from this truly tactless hermeneutic horror. When he receives Pip 'with open arms' and links 'his arm with mine', this is to share the 'homoerotic handling' of Pip by Magwitch. When Magwitch lies dying and Pip lays his hand lovingly on his breast and the old man puts both his hands on Pip, this is so clearly not a paedophiliac moment that even Cohen has to gloss it otherwise, even though he still can't get his fixed masturbatory notion out of his head ('Pip is capable of turning Magwitch's lecherous pawing back upon him, lending it a normalized, moralized signification'). Pip's last word to Magwitch is of Estella, her beauty, his love for her; and Magwitch 'raised my hand to his lips', with Pip's own help: which is explained by our Theorist interpreter as Pip's being 'at last able to translate his benefactor's uncomfortable stroking into heterosexual terms'. Clearly, Cohen's touch is for other things than those Dickens would have us be touched by. The way this reader's analysis can do no other than refuse to let itself be touched at the end of this novel, and the way it would not have any other reader be touched by it either, is enough to condemn it. But the whole discussion is a wrong handling, all, one might say, a pocketful of the wry and the awry – a wryly woeful mishandling of Dickens's lovely, careful, and most touching, trade in the meaning of hands, especially hands whose touching and joining, like Adam and Eve's in Milton's *Paradise Lost*, signify love and kinship and solidarity in a harsh world ('They hand in hand with wandering steps and slow, / Through Eden took their solitary way'). Given over to a large tactless insistence on his own Theory-compelled line – his large glop of loosely coherent Theory gumbo, freely spatchcocked together out of some post-Freudianism, some touches of Q, some cultural materialism, some neo-historicism, some large Pyrrhonist what-not – and there's more, much more where this came from – Cohen's mishandling of Dickens's hands is truly a marker of the absence of necessary tact in a highly Theorized reading, a marker, too, of the desperate need for tact to rescue reading from such going astray.[26]

The mishandling by two other Q Theorists of scenes of touching in a very touching poem of Gerard Manley Hopkins – and for my purposes, these are tellingly tactile failures not least because they're a mishandling of sacramental scenes – only endorses what I'm suggesting is a large failure of tact in Theory-compelled interpretations. Joseph Bristow's influential article of 1992, 'Hopkins and the Working-Class Male Body', busily outs the Jesuit–poet–priest as homosexually

159

infatuated with the bodies of proletarian males (though this particular closet door had been more than ajar for a long time). It's a good example of Q reading in particular and of Q Theory's project in general. The way, though, that Bristow handles Hopkins's sonnet 'Felix Randal', which is about the death of a blacksmith, one of Hopkins's Liverpool parishioners, is so tactless – and tactless, symptomatically, as I say, about tactility – as to be yet another parable of Theory's impulsion this way. In the poem the priest anoints the sick man, in a sacramental touch. He offers him the sweet food of the sacramental wafer ('since I had our sweet reprieve and ransom / Tendered to him'). There are other tender bodily exchanges too. The priest's touch dries the man's tears, the man's tears touch the priest's heart. But all the time the priest is wary, as Hopkins is in other poems, of the priestly touch turning into something less spiritual. And all of this tender realization in a poem of the lovely intimacy of priest and parishioner at the table of the Lord and on a deathbed, are simply swept away in Bristow's brusque talk of the priest's 'mastering' Felix Randal's body. A tactless roughness of reading only outdone by Greg Woods's own rough-and-ready critical tactlessness (in his *A History of Gay Literature: The Male Tradition*, 1998) in talking about the attractive 'sweat' of the blacksmith. There is of course no sweat in this poem. It's been imported gratuitously on the back of Theory's trundling lorry-load of stock notions.[27]

To really bring such Theory-led mis-handlings into focus, I take what I have to celebrate as a tact-full reading of a poem about a hand, by a renowned Theorist, but a reading done before Theory set in to turn this particular hermeneute's hand against the grain of the texts he contemplated. The poem is Keats's 'This Living Hand', a candidate for being the last poem from his hand.

> This living hand, now warm and capable
> Of earnest grasping, would, if it were cold
> And in the icy silence of the tomb,
> So haunt thy days and chill thy dreaming nights
> That thou wouldst wish thine own heart dry of blood
> So in my veins red life might stream again,

And thou be conscience-calmed – see here it is –
I hold it toward you.

It is a violently negative poem, in which the poet imagines his own demise in terms of the mortality of his still living hand, the hand that unites him with his living loved ones (Fanny Brawne especially?), the hand whose livingness holds the pen and is essential to the life of his poems. It is hardly a poem of blessing, more like a curse, a kind of malign proleptic elegy (When I'm dead, you'll regret not grasping the hand I now hold out to you). The offered hand is a warning, a threat – take it now, or else. The imagined tactility is edgy, on edge. Here's an imaginative grasp of human tactility in terms of the imagination's shocking ability to imagine its own mortality, the cold end of what it is grasping, the end of imaginative grasping itself. The offered hand is an offer of the cold hand of death, a coldness terribly implicit in the warmth of the still living hand. As human contacts go, this one is on the distinctly painful, negative, even morbid side. In terms of how human tactility might be accounted for, and appealed to, and used in human relationships, this poem's, this poet's, method and approach and usage seem, well, rather tactless. This is surely not how to win a lover over, you might say. So here, you might indeed also say, is an example of the self-deconstructing, self-cancelling poem – celebrating death in life, life in death; warmth in coldness, coldness in warmth; the offer of the living touch which is also the mortal touch, and vice versa; the offer of a hand which the recipient would, surely, hesitate to take up, in other words an offering that knows its own unwelcomeness, an offering which as it were withdraws itself even as it's being proposed. Here surely is *aporia*.

But that would, I think, be overdoing the reading. Somewhat tactlessly, if not totally tactlessly. After all, what's on offer is the still living hand; the dead hand is only made present in the *as if* world of imaginative possibility ('if it were cold . . .'). To apply the deconstructionist reading would indeed be the application of Theory's too chilling hand. And, arrestingly, Paul de Man, pre-Theory Paul de Man, Paul de Man on the cusp of the Theory he became renowned for, is more

161

tactful with this poem than he would later get with the very same Romantic materials he invokes in his extremely interesting discussion of the Keats.

This is in his Signet Classics edition, *The Selected Poems of Keats* (1966): Paul de Man writing on the threshold of Derrida's explosive arrival in the USA. His reading of the poem is the climax of his Introduction, his own last word, for the moment, on Keats. It rightly stresses the climactic negativity of the poem:

> After having acted, in all his dreams of human redemption, as the one who rescues others from their mortal plight, his last poem reverses the parts. Taking off from an innocuous line in *The Fall of Hyperion* ('When this warm scribe my hand is in the grave') he now offers his hand no longer in a gesture of assistance to others, but as the victim who defies another to take away from him the weight of his own death.

But, strikingly, in the light of de Man's vivid turn into deconstruction, which was about to happen even as this Introduction was being published, the stress is all – and touchingly so – on the moral subject of Keats's poem (and poems), the moral and emotional effects of the writing, on its generalizable truths, on what the reader might truly learn and be affected by in reading Keats.

> Romantic literature, at its highest moments, encompasses the greatest degree of generality in an experience that never loses contact with the individual self in which it originates. . . . Nowadays, we are less than ever capable of philosophical generality rooted in genuine self-insight, while our sense of selfhood hardly ever rises above self-justification. Hence that our criticism of romanticism so often misses the mark: for the great romantics, consciousness of self was the first and necessary step toward moral judgement. . . . [In Keats's last poems] he reached the same insight; the fact that he arrived at it by a negative road may make him all the more significant for us.

162

Individual self, philosophical generality, self-insight, consciousness of self, moral judgement, insight, significance for readers, poems with knowable meanings and moral effects that can be grasped or not ('missing the mark'): this could almost be Martha Nussbaum talking. The later Paul de Man is, it must be acknowledged, just glimpsable within this extremely tactful reading – this rather fine grasping of the hand 'This Living Hand' proffers. De Man's example of formative individual experience, granted general force by Romantic writers, is the originating act of youthful wrong-doing in Rousseau's *Confessions*, which 'awakened within him a universal moral sense'. De Man's obsession with Rousseau's guilt – now related by many to his own sense of youthful wrong-doing in collaborating with the Fascist cultural line in the Second World War – would feed into his later deconstructive phase and become a touchstone of the moral and personal and textual aporetics he espoused in his Theory-soaked Derridean years: readings showing far less touch, far less tact, for what is actually happening in Rousseau (and in Keats and the Romantics generally) than his glance here at the *Confessions* indicates. Theory had not yet arrived to confuse and blind his take on the text, to blunt his touch, and distance him (and his pupils) from it.[28]

Keats and Paul de Man are having a meeting of hands; they're in touch; the engagement is fruitfully tactile, tact-full. Which is to say, they are having a meeting, more or less, of minds. And that is, after all, and after all that Theory has clamoured to say, what reading a writing must be for. 'We're having a meeting of the minds.' That's Stephen King in his very biddable and down-to-earth autobiography-cum-How-to-Do-It book *On Writing* (2000). This is at the place where King discusses 'What Writing Is'. It's 'Telepathy, of course'. King hasn't, I'm pretty sure, read Derrida, nor even Nicholas Royle's Derridean *Telepathy and Literature: Essays on the Reading Mind* (1990). And I refuse to suggest, as Hillis Miller might, that King has read Derrida by unconscious telepathy or telepathic osmosis. King's telepathy, reading-as-telepathy, is thoroughly realistic: 'No mythymountain shit; real telepathy': an author speaking at long-distance in time and space to his unknown readers – a man writing, as he says, in

163

December 1997, but being read elsewhere and at a later date by someone out there. A real reader, not some 'mythy-mountain shit' ghostly
reader with no self before the message got to him (i.e. not a reader on
Hillis Miller's Derridean-ish plan). A reader who gets the message,
more or less, that King contrives by way of illustration of how this
telepathy works. 'I sent you a table with a red cloth on it, a cage, a
rabbit, and the number eight in blue ink' – this was the little picture
King asked his reader to 'see' – and 'You got them all, especially that
blue eight'. And, yes, I did.

Of course, King is not such a dumb cowpoke theorist of writing as
to believe that his readers will not vary in their readings and that his
red cloth and his rabbit cage won't strike people with some differences here and there. 'There will be necessary variations, of course:
some receivers will see a cloth which is turkey red. . . . Decorative
souls may add a little lace, and welcome – my tablecloth is your tablecloth, knock yourself out.' 'Likewise, the matter of the cage leaves
quite a lot of room for individual interpretation.' The point, though,
is that 'We all understand the cage is just a see-through medium'. And
the number eight on the rabbit's back is utterly clear: 'Not a six, not a
four, not nineteen-point five. It's an eight. This is what we're looking
at, and we all see it.' 'We're not even in the same year together, let
alone in the same room . . . except we are together. We're close.'[29]
Close reading. Person to person. Human, tactile, tactful. The mix
King expounds is by no means merely ruinous, gappy, aporetic; by no
means utterly univocal either. But what's sought by the writer and
more or less found by the willing reader, is something understood,
through proximity, the close-up contact, the tactful approach, on either side.

As René Girard once nicely put it: 'The truth is that only the individual human being can give us the recognition we all seek'.[30]

10

When I Can Read My Title Clear

What is tact? To hear true, along with forgiveness. Forgiveness: giving in addition, banking on what is there in order to revive, to give the depressed patient (that stranger withdrawing into his wound) a new start, and give him the possibility of a new encounter.

Julia Kristeva, *Black Sun: Depression and Melancholia*

One of the most moving vignettes in Janet Duitsman Cornelius's book on literacy and religion in the lives of American slaves, *'When I Can Read My Title Clear': Literacy, Slavery, and Religion in the Ante-Bellum South* (1991), is the story of Belle Myers Carothers, a slave who one day realized with great joy that she could actually read when she spelled out the hymn of the great eighteenth-century Calvinist poet Isaac Watts, 'When I Can Read My Title Clear'. (Alberto Manguel's extremely fine *A History of Reading* (1996) led me to it.) 'I found a Hymn book one day and spelled out, "When I Can Read My Title Clear". I was so happy when I saw that I could really read, that I ran around telling all the other slaves.' The story and Watts's hymn comprise Cornelius's epigraph. Here's the hymn:

> When I can read my title clear
> To mansions in the skies,
> I'll bid farewell to ev'ry fear,
> And wipe my weeping eyes.

Should earth against my soul engage,
And hellish darts be hurl'd,
Then I can smile at Satan's rage
And face a frowning world.

Let cares, like a wild deluge come,
And storms of sorrow fall;
May I but safely reach my home,
My God, my heav'n, my all:

There shall I bathe my weary soul,
In seas of heav'nly rest,
And not a wave of trouble roll
Across my peaceful breast.

The poem is a characteristic Calvinistic mixture of faith and hope and hesitation. The poet is not yet able to read his 'title clear' – not able to read with confidence the biblical title deed offering him possession of his heavenly mansion. He thinks the biblical promises are for him; suspects they should be for him (they are '*my* title'); but meanwhile their meanings are not yet being fully appropriated by him. But this is not at all the utter stymying of sense, the stoppage of really present meaning, of meaning apprehension, of the offer of the 'title' – such as are suggested as normal by the glib merchants of *aporia*. Watts's *when* is anticipatory of a hoped-for time when clear reading, absolute appropriation of the biblical promises, will arrive, when he will really, as it were, get his hands on the text's promise. There's a whole ethicity-in-hermeneutic present here, in potential at least. And meanwhile, wheels within wheels, Belle Myers Carothers has started to enter into this Watts world of strained but promising Bible reading, begun to read her own title clear to literacy, begun to grasp what literacy means, what kind of entitlement reading might be. Her realization is a powerful mix of, and release into, the hermeneutic, the ethical and the political. A set of clarities, emergent only from close-up encounters of the tactful-reading kind.

166

It's the desire of meaning-full, pleromatic, close-up, hands-on textual encounters of the sort occluded, sneered-at, cast into outer (or utter, utterance) darkness by Theory, which has animated the best resistances and reworkings of Theory ever since the News from Paris started to come in. And any argument, like mine, for what I'm calling tact in reading must pay tribute to all those readers whose exemplary practices in various sorts of close-reading (some of it travelling under the influence of Theory) kept the flag of the delicately human, text-respecting, text-loving and, yes, text-forgiving hermeneutic touch, flying through the Dark Days of Theory – the children so to say of William Empson and Donald Davie, the likes of Helen Vendler, and John Carey, John Hollander, Brian Vickers, Geoffrey Hill, Margaret Doody, Pat Rogers, David Nokes, Claude Rawson, Christine Brooke-Rose, Chris Baldick, Richard Friedman, Robert Alter, George Steiner, William H. Pritchard, Franco Moretti, Maud Ellmann, Patricia Parker, Phil Baker, Karl Miller, Tony Tanner, Christopher Prendergast, Stan Smith, Eric Griffiths, John Lennard, and, of course, Christopher Ricks especially, one of the finest close readers around. It pleases me very much indeed to find Ricks defending 'The Matter of Fact' in texts and in reading as not a matter of 'theory but rather of principle and tact'.[1]

The time of such readers is now, surely, come again. Symptomatic of this – highly symptomatic, I'd say – is Julian Wolfreys's *Readings: Acts of Close Reading in Literary Theory*, which I referred to earlier, his A–Z of Theory as revealed in a set of extracts from Theoretical writings given close scrutiny – very close scrutiny indeed. Here, for once, is a Theory text fulfilling the claim made by some Theory defenders – a claim not often enough fulfilled – that Theorists are truly close readers. And in practice, of course, what's happening in Wolfreys's book is that this Theory evangelist is actually advertising what all tactful readers have known all along, namely that all good and true reading is close reading; that no reading can claim the name which is not like that. It's a sign, I hope, of Theory coming to its senses. As exemplary, shall we say, as the later stages of Frank Kermode's career trajectory. The traditionalist reader of the text, not least of the Shakespearian text

167

(as his 1958 Arden edition of *The Tempest* indicated), Kermode was enticed by structuralism at the end of the 1960s when it came across the English Channel, as so many critics were. His criticism got dutifully inflected through linguistic models. He was persuaded to invest with great force in the sceptical possibilities deconstruction offered readers of canonical, classical texts (his deconstructionist reading of the Gospel of Mark, *The Genesis of Secrecy; On the Interpretation of Narrative*, 1979, was hugely influential as well as greatly symptomatic of the time). Kermode's good sense – call it critical tact – did, though, keep him holding on to the old, and British, tradition of interest in truth and value and reference, the old ethical–hermeneutical package, even as he was dunking into the more sceptical waters flowing from Paris and (to parody Chaucer) from Paris-atte-Yale (see his *The Classic* (1973), *Essays on Fiction 1971–1982* (1983), *Forms of Attention* (1985), *History and Value* (1989), *The Uses of Error* (1990)). And his book *Shakespeare's Language* (2000) has him returning to what he sees as the neglected text of Shakespeare as such, doing again a kind of purist Practical Critical job, out of impatience with 'the prevailing modes of Shakespeare criticism'. He means the modes sponsored by Theory, especially that sinking of questions of literary value 'in a context of political oppression and resistance' which characterizes New Historicism and Feminism and Postcolonialism and Queer Studies. Kermode's Bateson Memorial Lecture 2001 carries the theoretical (and practical) battle right up to the Theory gates – it was announced as 'An Exercise in Criticism Old Style', and declared very explicitly that the New-Historicist practice of parallel textualizing is actually an irrelevance when we come down to real textual appropriation.[2]

How, one might say, are the mighty not so much fallen, as come right round to sound sense. High Theorists will no doubt lament a falling away on the part of Kermode, a secession from the High Theoretical ground, and a lapse into an old-fashioned kind of empiricism and pragmatism, let alone into humanism and moralism, a return to a discreditable kind of common-sense vision of text and language and meaning by a now Lost Leader. Well, so be it. I myself prefer to think of this latest approach of his to Shakespeare's texts as a properly

168

cautioned post-Theory move, a rational, proper, moral even, respect for the primacy of text over all theorizing about text, a sensible recognition that though reading always comes after theory, theory is inevitably the lesser partner in the hermeneutic game. Readerly tact – or simply tact – should tell us that.

Notes

2 Reading Always Comes After

1 'Disagreeable to Unbearable' (7 July 1967), in *Reference Back: Philip Larkin's Uncollected Jazz Writings 1940–1984*, ed. Richard Palmer and John White (University of Hull Press, 1999), 75.
2 St Augustine, *Confessions*, trans. Henry Chadwick (Oxford World's Classics, 1992), chapter 8, 152–3. See Peter Brown, *Augustine of Hippo: A Biography* (Faber & Faber, 1967), chapter 10, 101ff.; and Alberto Manguel, *A History of Reading* (Harper Collins, 1996), 44–5.
3 John Milton, *De Doctrina Christiana*, first published in 1825; *Christian Doctrine*, trans. John Carey, in *Complete Prose Works of John Milton*, VI, *ca 1658–ca 1660* (Yale University Press, 1973), 583, 584.
4 Daniel Defoe, *Robinson Crusoe* (1719–26), ed. J. Donald Crowley (Oxford World's Classics, 1983), 221 (text based on 1719 version).
5 *Christian Doctrine*, 582; and notes 20, 21, 23, pp 582–4.
6 *The Mill on the Floss*, ed. Gordon S. Haight (Oxford World's Classics, 1996), 289–90. There seems little doubt that Maggie's experience with this book reflects George Eliot's own.
7 Harold Bloom, *How To Read And Why* (Fourth Estate, 2000), 120.

3 Theory, What Theory?

1 *Losing the Big Picture: The Fragmentation of the English Major Since 1964* (National Association of Scholars, Princeton, NJ, 2000).

2   For Gerard Genette, see 'Fiction and Diction' in his *Fiction and Diction*, trans. Catherine Porter (Cornell University Press, 1993), 1–29. For Hirsch and Fish, see Stanley Fish, 'Consequences' in W. J. T. Mitchell, ed., *Against Theory: Literary Studies and the New Pragmatism* (University of Chicago Press, 1985), 106–31.

3   John Sturrock, *The Word from Paris: Essays on Modern French Thinkers and Writers* (Verso, 1998).

4   'Structure, Sign, and Play in the Discourse of the Human Sciences': one version of the lecture is in Jacques Derrida, *Writing and Difference*, trans. Alan Bass (Routledge & Kegan Paul, 1978), 278–93.

5   Julian Wolfreys, 'Introduction', *Literary Theories: A Reader and Guide*, ed. J. Wolfreys (Edinburgh University Press, 1999), x–xi.

6   The best bibliography of Foucault's writings is in David Macey, *The Lives of Michel Foucault* (Hutchinson, 1993).

7   See Alan Sinfield, *Faultlines: Cultural Materialism and the Politics of Dissident Reading* (Clarendon Press, 1992).

8   Henry Louis Gates, Jr, 'Authority, (White) Power, and the (Black) Critic; or, it's all Greek to me', in Ralph Cohen, ed., *The Future of Literary Theory* (Routledge, 1989), 334.

9   'Gumbo, Jambalaya, and Other Classic Soups and Stews', in Howard Mitcham, *Creole Gumbo and All That Jazz: A New Orleans Seafood Cookbook* (Addison-Wesley Publishing, 1978), 39–40.

10   See Gates, *The Signifying Monkey: A Theory of African-American Literary Criticism* (Oxford University Press, 1988), 223.

11   See Derek Gregory, *Geographical Imaginations* (Blackwell Publishers, 1994).

12   Hayden White led the way, of course, with his *Metahistory: The Historical Imagination in Nineteenth-Century Europe* (Johns Hopkins University Press, 1973) and *The Content of the Form: Narrative Discourse and Historical Representation* (Johns Hopkins University Press, 1987). Typical is the mass of work on representations of the Holocaust, e.g. Dominick La Capra, *Representing the Holocaust: History, Theory, Trauma* (Cornell University Press, 1994).

13   See, for example, Philip Brett, Elizabeth Wood and Gary C. Thomas, eds, *Queering the Pitch: The New Gay and Lesbian Musicology* (Routledge, 1994); and Richard Dellamara and Daniel Fischlin, eds, *The Work of Opera: Genre, Nationhood, and Sexual Difference* (Columbia University Press, 1997).

171

14 See, for example, *The Bible and Culture Collective, The Postmodern Bible* (Yale University Press, 1995), which has a huge and most useful bibliography. For deconstruction and theology in particular, see Valentine Cunningham, 'The Rabbins Take It Up One After Another', in *In The Reading Gaol: Postmodernity, Texts, and History* (Blackwell Publishers, 1994), 363–410.

15 The large push of Theory into art history begins, I suppose, with Michel Foucault's inspection of Velasquez's *Las Meninas* in *Les Mots et les choses* (Editions Gallimard, 1966) – *The Order of Things: An Archaeology of the Human Sciences* (Tavistock Publications, 1966) – and Jaques Derrida's *La Verité en peinture* (Flammarion, 1978) – *The Truth in Painting*, trans. Geoff Bennington and Ian McLeod (Chicago University Press, 1987) – and Roland Barthes's *La Chambre claire* (Editions du Seuil, 1980) – *Camera Lucida: Reflections on Photography*, trans. Richard Howard (Cape, 1982).

16 See, for example, Stanley Fish, *Doing What Comes Naturally: Change, Rhetoric, and the Practice of Theory in Literary and Legal Studies* (Clarendon Press, 1989), and Maria Aristodemou, *Law and Literature: Journeys from Her to Eternity* (Oxford University Press, 2000).

17 Any one of the numerous exhibitions on medical history, anatomy, the business of reading the body in history and in the present which have become so commonplace through the 1990s tells this story well. I was very impressed by *The Quick and the Dead* travelling exhibition and its catalogue under that title, ed. Deanna Petherbridge (Hayward Gallery/ Arts Council, 1997).

18 Alan D. Sokal, 'Transgressing the Boundaries: Towards a Transformative Hermeneutics of Quantum Gravity', *Social Text* 46/47, vol. 14, nos 1 and 2, Spring/Summer 1996, 217–52. See also Sokal's outrage at the ease of his deception: 'A Physicist Experiments With Cultural Studies', *Lingua Franca*, May/June 1996.

19 Douglas Tallack, ed., *Literary Theory at Work: Three Texts* (B. T. Batsford, 1987).

20 Julian Wolfreys, 'Introduction: Border Crossings, or Close Encounters of the Textual Kind', in *Literary Theories*, 1–11.

21 'Philosophy Without Principles', in *Against Theory: Literary Studies and the New Pragmatism*, ed. W. J. T. Mitchell (University of Chicago Press, 1985), 132.

22 The wonderfully wide-ranging *Cambridge History of Literary Criticism*, Vol. 3, *The Renaissance*, ed. Glyn P. Norton (Cambridge University

Press, 1999) is most informative on the Renaissance relation with the classical forebears. For the ancient materials, see: Aristotle, *Poetics*, trans. Richard Janko (Hackett Publishing, 1987); *Ancient Literary Criticism: The Principal Texts in New Translations*, ed. D. A. Russell and M. Winterbottom (Clarendon Press, 1972); and D. A. Russell, *Criticism in Antiquity* (Duckworth, 1981).

23 'Of Dramatic Poesy: An Essay' (1668): in the good collection of Dryden's critical writings, *Of Dramatic Poesy and Other Critical Essays*, 2 vols, ed. George Watson (Everyman's Library, Dent, 1962). See Michael Werth Gelber, *The Just and the Lively: The Literary Criticism of John Dryden* (Manchester University Press, 1999), and Thomas Docherty, 'Tragedy and the Nationalist Condition of Criticism', in his *Criticism and Modernity: Aesthetics, Literature, and Nations in Europe and its Academies* (Oxford University Press, 1999).

24 See Samuel Johnson, 'The Life of Milton' in the *Lives of the Poets* (1783), and his 'Notes on King Lear', in any gathering of Johnson's work, e.g. *Rasselas, Poems, and Selected Prose*, ed. Bertrand H. Bronson (Holt, Rinehart and Winston, 1958). H. R. Woudhuysen, ed., *Samuel Johnson on Shakespeare* (Penguin Books, 1989) is excellent.

25 See, for example, Allen Reddick, *The Making of Johnson's Dictionary 1746–1773* (Cambridge University Press, 1990).

26 See Wolfgang Iser, *The Fictive and the Imaginary: Charting Literary Anthropology* (Johns Hopkins University Press, 1993); and *The Anthropological Turn in Literary Studies*, ed. Jürgen Schlaeger: *Real: Yearbook of Research in English and American Literature*, Vol. 12 (Gunter Narr Verlag, 1996).

27 See *Representations of Emotional Excess*, ed. Jürgen Schlaeger: *Real: Yearbook of Research in English and American Literature*, Vol. 16 (Gunter Narr Verlag, 2000).

28 Peter Ackroyd, *Dickens* (Sinclair-Stevenson, 1995); Richard Holmes, *Dr Johnson and Mr Savage* (Hodder & Stoughton, 1993). See John Batchelor, ed., *The Art of Literary Biography* (Clarendon Press, 1989), and Paula R. Backsheider, *Reflections on Biography* (Oxford University Press, 2001).

4   The Good of Theory

1   See Wolfgang Iser, *Sterne, Tristram Shandy*, trans. David Henry Wilson (Landmarks of World Literature, Cambridge University Press, 1988).
2   F. R. Leavis, *The Great Tradition: George Eliot, Henry James, Joseph Conrad* (Chatto & Windus, 1948).
3   For a fine argument about the need to revalue popular/female/senti-mental work in the shape of Harriet Beecher Stowe's *Uncle Tom's Cabin*, see Jane Tompkins, 'Sentimental Power: *Uncle Tom's Cabin* and the Politics of Literary History', in her *Sensational Designs: The Cultural Work of American Fiction 1790–1860* (Oxford University Press, 1985).
4   Roger Lonsdale, ed., *Eighteenth-Century Women Poets: An Oxford Anthology* (Oxford University Press, 1989).
5   J. Hillis Miller, 'The Function of Literary Theory at the Present Time', in Ralph Cohen, ed., *The Future of Literary Theory* (Routledge, 1989), 109.
6   Elaine Showalter, 'A Criticism Of Our Own: Autonomy and Assimila-tion in Afro-American and Feminist Literary Theory', in Cohen, *The Future of Literary Theory*, 347–69.
7   Henry Louis Gates, Jr., 'Authority, (White) Power, and the (Black) Critic', in *The Future of Literary Theory*, 345.
8   See, for example, Gayatri Chakravorty Spivak, *In Other Worlds: Essays in Cultural Politics* (Methuen, 1987), *passim*, but especially 95–102; 103ff.; 134ff.
9   Eve Kosofsky Sedgwick, *Tendencies* (Routledge, 1994), 9, 110ff.: 'Queer and Now' (first in *Wild Orchids and Trotsky: Messages from American Universities*, 1993), and 'Jane Austen and the Masturbating Girl' (first in *Critical Inquiry*, Summer 1991).
10 Julian Barnes, *Flaubert's Parrot* (1984); Picador edition (1985), 84.

5   Fragments . . . Ruins

1   'Before the Law', trans. Christine Roulston, in *Jacques Derrida: Acts of Literature*, ed. Derek Attridge (Routledge, 1992), 183–220.
2   Catherine Gallagher and Stephen Greenblatt, *Practicing New Historicism* (Chicago University Press, 2000), 4.

3 See 'The Wound in the Wall', ibid., 76ff.

4 Michel de Montaigne, 'Apologie de Raimond Sebond', *Essais*, ed. Pierre Michel (Gallimard, 1965), Book II, ch. xii, 252–3. *The Complete Essays*, trans. and ed. M. A. Screech (Allen Lane, 1991), 590–95.

5 Walter Benjamin, 'Allegory and Trauerspiel', in *The Origin of German Tragic Drama* [*Ursprung des deutschen Trauerspiels*, 1963], trans. John Osborne (New Left Books, 1977), 178.

6 Paul de Man, 'Allegory as De-facement', in *The Rhetoric of Romanticism* (Columbia University Press, 1984).

7 Stephen Greenblatt, in Gallagher and Greenblatt, *Practicing New Historicism*, 82.

8 Nicholas Royle, *After Derrida* (Manchester University Press, 1995), 168–9; reprinted in J. Wolfreys, ed., *Literary Theories: A Reader and Guide* (Edinburgh University Press, 1999), 305.

9 John Milton, *De Doctrina Christiana*, first published in 1825; *Christian Doctrine*, trans. John Carey, in *Complete Prose Works of John Milton*, VI, *ca 1658–ca 1660* (Yale University Press, 1973), Bk I, ch. 30, 580.

10 Geoffrey Hartman, *The Fate of Reading, And Other Essays* (University of Chicago Press, 1975), 14.

6 All What Jazz? Or, The Incredibly Disappearing Text

1 Terence Hawkes, 'Telmah', in, for example, his *That Shakespeherean Rag: Essays on a Critical Process* (Methuen, 1986), 92–119.

2 Stanley Fish, 'How to Recognize a Poem When You See One', in *Is There A Text in This Class? The Authority of Interpretive Communities* (Harvard University Press, 1980), 322–37.

3 Raymond Tallis, in *The Arts and Sciences of Criticism*, ed. David Fuller and Patricia Waugh (Oxford University Press, 1999), 87.

4 Stanley Fish, 'No Bias, No Merit: The Case Against Blind Submission', in *Doing What Comes Naturally: Change, Rhetoric, and the Practice of Theory in Literary and Legal Studies* (Clarendon Press, 1989), 169; and *Professional Correctness: Literary Studies and Political Change* (Clarendon Press, 1995), 13.

5 Stanley Fish, 'Literature in the Reader', in *Is There A Text in This Class?*, 43.

6   Stephen Grenblatt, *Shakespearian Negotiations: The Circulation of Social Energy in Renaissance England* (Clarendon Press, 1988).

7   Timocracy was that Greek form of rule by people who have acquired and manifest certain kinds of personal property, money, moral merit, military honour: see *timokratia, timokratikos* in J. O. Urmson, *The Greek Philosophical Vocabulary* (Duckworth, 1990), 169; and the OED.

8   Stephen Greenblatt, *Learning to Curse: Essays in Early Modern Culture* (Routledge, 1990), 80ff.

9   See, for example, Frank Kermode, *The Classic: Literary Images of Permanence and Change* (1975; expanded edn, Harvard University Press, 1983).

10 See Valentine Cunningham, *In the Reading Gaol: Texts, Postmodernity and History* (Blackwell Publishers, 1994), 363ff.

11 See, for example, Harold Bloom, *The Breaking of the Vessels* (University of Chicago Press, 1982), and *Ruin the Sacred Truths: Poetry and Belief from the Bible to the Present* (Harvard University Press, 1989); Walter Benjamin, 'The Task of the Translator', trans. in *Illuminations*, ed. Hannah Arendt (Cape, 1970); René Girard, *Violence and the Sacred*, trans. Patrick Gregory (Johns Hopkins University Press, 1977), and *Le Bouc émissaire* (Grasset, 1982); Michel Serres, *The Parasite*, trans. Lawrence R. Scher (Johns Hopkins University Press, 1982); Susan Handelman, *The Slayers of Moses: the Emergence of Rabbinic Interpretation in Modern Literary Theory* (State University of New York Press, 1982); Robert Eaglestone, *Ethical Criticism After Levinas* (Edinburgh University Press, 1997).

12 Jorge Luis Borges, 'The Mirror of Enigmas', in *Labyrinths*, ed. Donald A. Yates and James E. Irly (Penguin Books, 1971), 246–7.

13 See Cunningham, *In the Reading Gaol*, 33–5.

14 Tzvetan Todorov, 'Saussure's Semiotics', in *Theories of the Symbol*, trans. Catherine Porter (Blackwell Publishers, 1977), 255–70.

15 Frank Kermode, 'Can We Say Absolutely Anything We Like?' (1976), in *The Art of Telling: Essays on Fiction* (Harvard University Press, 1983).

16 'Hoffman's Tale', *Guardian Saturday Review* (28 April 2001), 7.

17 Paul Muldoon, *To Ireland, I: The Clarendon Lectures in English Literature 1998* (Oxford University Press, 2000), 45–9, 109, et passim!

18 Geoffrey Hartman, 'The State of the Art of Criticism', in Ralph Cohen, ed., *The Future of Literary Theory* (Routledge, 1989), 97–8.

19 I. A. Richards, *Practical Criticism: A Study of Literary Judgement* (1929; 3rd impression, Kegan Paul Trübner, 1935), 110, 111, 160.

20 Umberto Eco, with Richard Rorty, Jonathan Culler, Christine Brooke-

Rose, *Interpretation and Overinterpretation*, ed. Stefan Collini (Cambridge University Press, 1992), 141, 144, 146, 151.

21 Gerard Graff, *Literature Against Itself: Literary Ideas in Modern Society* (Chicago University Press, 1979), 204.

22 Jacques Lacan, re: 'Booz Endormi' in 'From Interpretation to The Transference', *The Four Concepts of Psychoanalysis*, ed. Jacques-Alain Miller, trans. Alan Sheridan (Penguin Books, 1979), 247ff.

7 Textual Abuse: Or, Down With Stock Responses

1 William A. Cohen, *Sex Scandal: The Private Parts of Victorian Fiction* (Duke University Press, 1996).

2 Malcolm Bowie, 'Jacques Lacan', in *Structuralism and Since: From Lévi-Strauss to Derrida*, ed. John Sturrock (Oxford University Press, 1979), 116.

3 See Quentin Skinner, ed., *The Return of Grand Theory in the Human Sciences* (Cambridge University Press, 1985).

4 Roland Barthes, *S/Z* (Éditions du Seuil, 1970), 11. My translation.

5 Sandra Gilbert and Susan Gubar, 'The Mirror and the Vamp: Reflections on Feminist Criticism', in *The Future of Literary Theory* (Routledge, 1989), 144–66.

6 Barthes, *S/Z*, 20–1. Cf. his *malmener*: reviling, maltreating the text.

7 J. Hillis Miller, 'The Critic as Host', in *Theory Now and Then* (Harvester Wheatsheaf, 1991), 143–70; Homi Bhabha, 'Articulating the Archaic', in *The Location of Culture* (Routledge, 1994), 136–7.

8 Paul de Man, '"Conclusions": Walter Benjamin's "The Task of the Translator"', in *The Resistance to Theory* (Manchester University Press, 1991), 73–105.

9 For more, see Valentine Cunningham, 'Sticky Transfers', in *Aesthetics and Contemporary Discourse, Real 10*, ed. Herbert Grabes (Gunter Narr Verlag, 1994), 336ff.; Stanley Corngold, 'Error in Paul de Man', *Critical Inquiry* 8 (Spring 1982), 489–513; Brian Vickers, *In Defence of Shakespeare* (Clarendon Press, 1988), 454–7.

10 It's in Peggy Kamuf, ed., *A Derrida Reader: Between the Blinds* (Columbia University Press, 1991), 270–6; and in J. Wolfreys, ed., *Literary Theories: A Reader and Guide* (Edinburgh University Press, 1999), 282–7.

11   I. A. Richards, *Practical Criticism*, 16–17.

12   I. A. Richards, *Principles of Literary Criticism* (Routledge and Kegan Paul, 1924; Routledge paperback, 1960), ch. 9, 63ff.

13   Julia Kristeva, *The Black Sun: Depression and Melancholia*, trans. Leon S. Roudiez (Columbia University Press, 1989), 203.

14   Harold Bloom, *How To Read and Why* (Fourth Estate, 2000), 167.

15   Richard Rorty, 'The Contingency of Selfhood', in *Contingency, Irony and Solidarity* (Cambridge University Press, 1989), 23ff. Rorty's depressing rushes to bad critical judgement are nicely illustrated by his wilfully shallow lists of writings that *stimulate* as oppose to *relax*: ibid., n. 3, 143. I agree utterly with Richard Lansdown's scathing demolition of these weird listings ('can we really believe that *Middlemarch* has nothing to offer in the way of relaxation, or that either it or *King Lear* provide "novel stimulus to action"?'). See R. Lansdown, *The Autonomy of Literature* (Macmillan, 2001), 56.

16   Terry Eagleton, *William Shakespeare* (Blackwell Publishers, 1986), 64.

17   Stanley Fish, 'Yet Once More', in *Professional Correctness: Literary Studies and Political Change* (Clarendon Press, 1995), 1–17.

18   See David Lehman, *Signs of the Times: Deconstruction and the Fall of Paul de Man* (André Deutsch, 1991).

19   Karl Marx, *Capital: A Critique of Political Economy*, Vol. 1, intro. Ernest Mandel, trans. Ben Fowkes (Penguin Books, 1976), 169.

20   Chinua Achebe, 'An Image of Africa: Racism in Conrad's *Heart of Darkness*', *The Massachusetts Review*, 18 (1977), 782–94; reprinted as a standard critical item in the Norton edition of *Heart of Darkness*, ed. Robert Kimbrough (W. W. Norton, 1988).

21   Edward Said, *Culture and Imperialism* (Chatto & Windus, 1993), 81–2.

22   Catharine R. Stimpson, 'Woolf's Room, Our Project: The Building of Feminist Criticism', in R. Cohen, ed., *The Future of Literary Criticism*, 134, 136. *A Room of One's Own* (Hogarth Press, 1929), ch. 3, 76.

23   Jacques Lacan, 'The Agency of the Letter in the Unconscious or Reason since Freud', in *Écrits: A Selection*, trans. Alan Sheridan (Tavistock, 1977), 147–59. Jacques Berthoud, 'Science and the Self: Lacan's Doctrine of the Signifier', in *The Arts and Sciences of Criticism*, ed. David Fuller and Patricia Waugh (Oxford University Press, 1999), 110–13.

24   Jacques Derida, 'Shibboleth', trans. Joshua Wilmer, in Geoffrey Hartman and Sanford Budick, eds, *Midrash and Literature* (Yale University Press, 1986), 307–47.

25   Stephen Greenblatt, 'The Wound in the Wall', in Catherine Gallagher and Stephen Greenblatt, *Practicing New Historicism* (Chicago University Press, 2000), 75–109.

26   Catherine Gallagher, 'The Potato in the Materialist Imagination', in Gallagher and Greenblatt, *Practicing New Historicism*, especially 114ff. The extent of Gallagher's awful misquotings and trenchant misreading of Cobbett can be measured by comparing it with *Cobbett in Ireland: A Warning to England*, ed. Denis Knight (Lawrence & Wishart, 1984), 82–3.

27   E. P. Thompson, *The Poverty of Theory and Other Essays* (Merlin Press, 1978), 300. It's quoted by Robert D. Hume, *Reconstructing Texts: The Aims and Principles of Archaeo-Historicism* (Clarendon Press, 1999), 106.

28   Thomas Hardy, 'The Torn Letter', in *The Complete Poems*, ed. James Gibson (Macmillan, 1976), 313–14.

29   J. Hillis Miller, 'Thomas Hardy, Jacques Derrida, and the "Dislocation of Souls"', in his *Tropes, Parables, Performatives* (Duke University Press, 1991), 171–80; excerpted in Wolfreys's *Literary Theories*, 288–97, as a choice example of deconstructive reading – which is why I chose to talk about it.

30   I take all these awful examples of Beckett traducing, and the Beckett passages I quote, from Christopher Ricks, *Beckett's Dying Words* (Clarendon Press, 1993), 148–51, whose fine critical anger over these lapdogs of Theory I utterly share and endorse.

8   Theory Shrinks

1   See for example Northrop Frye, *The Anatomy of Criticism* (Princeton University Press, 1957).

2   Vladimir Propp, *The Morphology of the Folktale*, 2nd revd edn, trans. Laurence Scott, ed. Louis A. Wagner (University of Texas Press, 1968), 65.

3   Jacques Derrida, 'Letter to a Japanese Friend', in *A Derrida Reader: Between the Blinds*, ed. Peggy Kamuf (Columbia University Press, 1991), 270–6.

4   Propp, *The Morphology of the Folktale*, 99.

5   Roland Barthes, 'Center-City, Empty Center', *Empire of Signs* [*L'Empire des signes*, 1970], trans. Richard Howard (Jonathan Cape, 1983), 34–5.

6   They're reproduced in, for example, Michael Sadleir, *Trollope: A Commentary* (1927; 3rd edn, Oxford University Press, 1961).
7   John Butt and Kathleen Tillotson, *Dickens at Work* (1957; Methuen, 1968), 142–3.
8   Vladimir Nabokov, *Lectures on Literature*, ed. Fredson Bowers, intro. John Updike (Weidenfeld & Nicolson, 1980).
9   James Fenton, *On Statues* (Penguin Books, 1995).
10 Iris Murdoch, 'Against Dryness', *Encounter*, January 1961; reprinted in Iris Murdoch, *Existentialists and Mystics: Writings on Philosophy and Literature*, ed. Peter Conradi (Chatto & Windus, 1997), 287–95.
11 Originally in *Los anales de Buenos Aires* (1946), then in *Historia universal de la infamia* (Buenos Aires, 1954): *A Universal History of Infamy*, trans. Norman Thomas di Giovanni (Penguin Books, 1973).
12 Jean Baudrillard, *Simulations*, trans. Paul Foss, Paul Patton and Philip Beitchman (Semiotext[e], Columbia University, 1983), 1ff.
13 Claude Lévi-Strauss, 'Structure and Form: Reflections on a Work by Vladimir Propp', in *Structural Anthropology* Vol. 2, trans. Monique Layton (Penguin Books, 1978), 115–45. The argument is discussed, with rather different emphases, but ones still pertinent to the issues raised here, in Valentine Cunningham, *In the Reading Gaol: Postmodernity, Texts, and History* (Blackwell Publishers 1994), 163–4.

9   Touching Reading

1   Italo Calvino, 'Why Read the Classics?', in *Why Read the Classics?*, trans. Martin McLaughlin (Jonathan Cape, 1999), 6.
2   Catharine A. Stimpson, 'Woolf's Room, Our Project: The Building of Feminist Criticism', in Ralph Cohen, ed., *The Future of Literary Theory* (Routledge, 1989), 137.
3   See Michael Riffaterre, 'Undecidability as Hermeneutic Constraint', in *Literary Theory Today*, ed. Peter Collier and Helga Geyer-Ryan (Polity Press, 1990), 109–23.
4   Ihab Hassan, *Selves at Risk: Patterns of Quest in Contemporary American Letters* (University of Wisconsin Press, 1990), 15; and Jerzy Durczak, 'Ihab Hassan: The Art of Risk', in *Anglistik* 11, 2 (September 2000), ed. Rüdiger Ahrens (C. Winter, 2000), 34–44.
5   Lisa Jardine, 'Saxon Violence', the *Guardian* (London, 8 December 1992).

See Valentine Cunningham, 'Canons', in *The Discerning Reader: Christian Perspectives on Literature and Theory*, ed. David Barratt, Roger Pooley and Leland Ryken (Apollos and Baker Books, 1995), 37–52.

6   Shoshana Felman, 'After the Apocalypse: Paul de Man and the Fall to Silence', in Shoshana Felman and Dori Laub, eds, *Testimony: Crises of Witnessing in Literature, Psychoanalysis, and History* (Routledge, 1994), 120–64.

7   Roland Barthes, *S/Z* (Editions du Seuil, 1970), 26–7.

8   Roland Barthes, 'The Struggle With the Angel: Textual Analysis of Genesis 32: 23–33', in, for example, *The Semiotic Challenge*, trans. Richard Howard (Blackwell Publishers, 1988), 246–60.

9   Roland Barthes, *Barthes par Barthes* (Editions du Seuil, 1975): *Barthes by Barthes*, trans. Richard Howard (Hill & Wang, 1977); *Le Grain de la voix: entretiens 1962–1980* (Editions du Seuil, 1981). See also *Incidents*, trans. Richard Howard (University of California Press, 1992).

10   Roland Barthes, *Sade/Fourier/Loyola* (1971), trans. Richard Miller (Hill & Wang, 1976).

11   For clear expression of this see the series editors' preface by Simon Critchley and Richard Kearney in Jacques Derrida, *On Forgiveness*, trans. Mark Dooley and Michael Hughes (Thinking in Action series, Routledge, 2001).

12   Czeslaw Milosz, *The Collected Poems (1931–1987)* (Penguin Books, 1988), 234.

13   Martha Nussbaum, *The Fragility of Goodness: Luck and Ethics in Greek Tragedy and Philosophy* (Cambridge University Press, 1986), 378ff.

14   Harold Bloom, *How to Read, and Why* (Fourth Estate, 2000), 73, 213.

15   Calvino, *Why Read the Classics?*, 7.

16   See Hans-Georg Gadamer, *Truth and Method* (Sheed & Ward, 1975), originally *Wahrheit und Methode: Grundzüge einer philosophischen Hermeneutik*, 2nd edn (Mohr, 1965).

17   See Coleridge in *The Romantics on Shakespeare*, ed. Jonathan Bate (Penguin Books, 1992); and Harold Bloom, *Shakespeare: The Invention of the Human* (Fourth Estate, 1999), more or less passim.

18   See Iris Murdoch, *The Sovereignty of Good* (Routledge, 1970). See also Peter Conradi's gathering of Iris Murdoch pieces, *Existentialists and Mystics* (Chatto & Windus, 1997), which includes other key Murdoch essays, e.g. 'The Sublime and the Good' and 'The Sublime and the Beautiful Revisited'.

181

19   See Martha Nussbaum, 'Flawed Crystals: James's *Golden Bowl* and Literature as Moral Philosophy', *New Literary History* 15 (1983), 24–50; and 'Perceptive Equilibrium: Literary Theory and Ethical Theory', in Cohen, *The Future of Literary Theory*, 58–85.

20   Daniel Defoe, *Robinson Crusoe*, ed. J. Donald Crowley (World's Classics, Oxford University Press, 1983), 113.

21   The whole poem is in Desmond Graham, ed., *Poetry of the Second World War: An International Anthology* (Chatto & Windus, 1995), 70–1.

22   John Milton, *Of Reformation . . .*, *Complete Prose Works of John Milton, Vol. 1, 1624–1642*, ed. Don M. Wolfe (Yale University Press and Oxford University Press, 1953), 547–8.

23   Roland Barthes, 'The World of Wrestling', in *Mythologies* (1957), trans. Annette Lavers (Cape,1972); and 'The Struggle With the Angel'.

24   D. H. Lawrence, 'Morality and the Novel', in *Phoenix: The Posthumous Papers of D. H. Lawrence*, ed. Edward D. McDonald (William Heinemann, 1936), 527–32.

25   In W. J. T. Mitchell, ed., *Against Theory: Literary Studies and the New Pragmatism* (University of Chicago Press, 1985), 107.

26   See William A. Cohen, *Sex Scandal: The Private Parts of Victorian Fiction* (Duke University Press, 1996), ch. 2, 26–72. I really do hope, by the way, that when in a footnote Cohen points to more 'homoerotic' Dickensian handshakes, and refers to the place in *Edwin Drood* where onetime schoolfriends Crisparkle and Tartar meet again and shake hands and lay their hands on each other's shoulders, he doesn't think Crisparkle's 'My old fag!' means 'My old faggot', i.e. homosexual in the American sense. Though Cohen seems to think that. See Cohen, *Sex Scandal*, n. 28, p. 47.

27   I discuss these readings and the poem at greater length in 'Fact and Tact', *Essays in Criticism* 51: 1, January 2001, 119–38.

28   Paul de Man, 'Introduction', *The Selected Poetry of Keats*, ed. Paul de Man (Signet Classics, New American Library, July 1966), ix–xxxvi. Compare 'Excuses (Confessions)', in *Allegories of Reading: Figural Language in Rousseau, Nietzsche, Rilke, and Proust* (Yale University Press, 1979), 278–303.

29   Stephen King, *On Writing* (New English Library, Hodder & Stoughton, 2000), 116–17.

30   René Girard, 'Theory and its Terrors', in *The Limits of Theory*, ed. Thomas Kavanagh (Stanford University Press, 1989), 246.

10   When I Can Read My Title Clear

1   Christopher Ricks, 'The Matter of Fact', in *Essays in Appreciation* (Oxford University Press, 1996), 283. See also his 'Principles as Against Theory', in ibid., 311–32. Naming names is invidious, and I name just a few, but I do it partly encouraged by J. Hillis Miller's notorious naming of his allies and admirees in his 1986 MLA Presidential Address, 'The Triumph of Theory, the Resistance to Reading, and the Question of the Material Base', reprinted in his *Theory Now and Then* (Harvester Wheatsheaf, 1991).
2   'Literary Criticism: Old and New Style', *Essays in Criticism*, vol. 10, no. 2 (April 2001), 191–207.

Index

186

190

Index

Index

194